Work for Yourself...
and Reap the Rewards

How to master your destiny and

be your own boss

Second edition

BRIAN ISAACS

howto books

Published by How To Books Ltd,
3 Newtec Place, Magdalen Road,
Oxford OX4 1RE. United Kingdom.
Tel: (01865) 793806. Fax: (01865) 248780.
email: info@howtobooks.co.uk
http://www.howtobooks.co.uk

First published 2002
Second edition 2004

British Library Cataloguing in Publication Data
A catalogue record for this book is available from the British
Library

Produced for How To Books by Deer Park Productions,
Tavistock
Edited by Diana Brueton
Typeset by PDQ Typesetting, Newcastle-under-Lyme, Staffs.
Cover design by Baseline Arts Ltd, Oxford
Printed and bound by Cromwell Press, Trowbridge, Wiltshire

NOTE: The material contained in this book is set out in good
faith for general guidance and no liability can be accepted
for loss or expense incurred as a result of relying in particular
circumstances on statements made in the book. The laws and
regulations are complex and liable to change, and readers should
check the current position with the relevant authorities before
making personal arrangements.

Contents

Preface

Walk into any library or bookshop and you will find numerous books on the subject of starting and operating your own
business. But there is no quick fix or easy way, and cutting
corners can lead to financial ruin. Caution and planning are
the keywords. This book is intended to guide the reader over
the many hurdles and obstacles associated with planning and
running a business in the modern world. Over half a million
new businesses are kick-started each year. Retired people,
redundant workers, housewives, disabled people, college-
or school-leavers and people who are simply sick of being
pushed around in a dead-end job. All have one thing in
common: the desire to work for themselves or be master
of their own destiny.

A high percentage of new businesses fail, mainly in the first
two years. With the right advice and planning, the reader will
recognise the pitfalls and be equipped to avoid them.

Over three million in the UK are self-employed, with the
largest sector being retail: the butcher, the baker and the
candlestick maker. So why are many independent retailers
struggling? The following trends may give us a clue:

- out-of-town shopping centres
- inadequate parking facilities
- supermarket produce diversification
- online shopping
- traffic congestion in towns.

These and many other reasons have seen the decline of the small independent retailer, but in my opinion by far the largest single reason and one that can easily be avoided is the mix of shops in our high streets. Let me explain.

Twenty-five years ago the high street was the best place to shop, because you were able to purchase your essentials as well as your luxury items there. Just down the road were a number of cinemas, perhaps even a bingo hall for the weary shopper to relax in. The high street was a meeting place, the focal point, the hub of the town. Not so today; too many shops have been allowed to change to non-retail use such as building societies, banks and travel agents, to mention just a few.

My town, Leigh-on-Sea in Essex, has gone against the trend. A good mix of shops, many of them independent traders, has created a shopping environment which is the envy of the surrounding towns. Location, then, requires a great deal more thought than just the availability of low-priced premises and we will be investigating some of the problem areas the reader may experience later in the book.

Whatever kind of business you are planning, honest self assessment is a good place to start. You may not like the answers, but they will urge you to question your ability as well as your motives. In Chapter 1 I will set out the criteria for becoming a successful small-business owner. In Chapter 2 you will test yourself to see how closely your profile matches those criteria. I have no intention of giving false hope; you will be made aware of the downside as well as the benefits of self-employment.

From Chapter 3 onwards, we look at the essential practical-
ities that you'll need to get to grips with. Each chapter of this
book is an entity in itself, to enable the reader to target
sections that apply to their proposed business. At the
same time, I have attempted to cross-reference where necessary. Use the Contents page to locate the points that concern
you.

One last thing: economic forecasts of doom and gloom can be
heard every time you turn on the television. But change chan-
nel and Del-boy will tell you 'who dares wins' – a catchphrase
well worth remembering as you formulate your business ideas.

Brian Isaacs

Acknowledgements

The author gratefully acknowledges the help, guidance, expertise and patience of the following people: first of all my wife for her kindness, patience and understanding, not to mention her proof reading ability, my 10-year-old daughter Clare for correcting my spelling mistakes and lending me her computer. Rob Bysouth MIBA, a veritable mine of experience with an undying desire to assist others. For their help with my research, Michael Spoor BSc (Eng), FIEE, MIMct, MIBA and all the staff at the Business Enterprise Agency of South East Essex. My accountant, Paul Stafford MAAT ACCA. David Horsley, general secretary of the South Essex Chamber of Commerce, and all my sponsors. My friend Brian (Bilge) Phillips, an inspiration to all who know him (if ever technology becomes capable of business acumen transplants, I want his). Last, but not least, my barber and friend, Elliot Baker, a rising star in the commercial world whose business tips are 100% better than his dreadful corny jokes.

(1)

Your Own Business: Reality or Just a Pipe Dream?

A BOLT OF LIGHTNING

Ingredient number one has to be an idea, or more to the point, the idea of starting a business. In many cases the thought doesn't evolve, it strikes like a bolt of lightning: you start to ask yourself why you had not considered it before. The place and time your idea hit you is likely to remain in your memory bank forever. So there you are, lying in bed at 2.30 a.m., unable to sleep, turning the plan over in your mind and waiting for the chance to bounce it off somebody to get their reaction and hopefully the encouragement to progress. It's a good time not to kill off the idea, but to start to plan a controlled development.

In my years as a business advisor for the Enterprise Agency, a good percentage of my time has been spent with first-time start-up businesses, in some instances attempting to stop people investing their life savings or their redundancy money into a business plan that is fatally flawed. I recall one lady about to invest £30,000, all the money she possessed in the world, in a short-term lease of a business that had already failed twice in the hands of experienced business people, something this lady was not. I was relieved when, two days after our meeting, the lady phoned to tell me she would not be pursuing the matter any further. To me that is as much a success as witnessing one of my clients strike it rich with a business plan the Enterprise Agency has helped hone and nurture to success. That lady did the right thing, she tapped into the free advice available and acted upon it. Others unfortunately suffer from the Lemming Syndrome: here's a cliff, let's throw ourselves over it.

To make a success of a new business venture demands a certain type of person. The ability to spot the right product and the right market at the right time is just as much a gift as a musical talent or an artistic flair. It is impossible to define the characteristics in advance of those destined for entrepreneurial stardom, but it is possible to give you some broad similarities. Here is my definition of an entrepreneur:

> **An entrepreneur is a person who is able to recognise a business opportunity, raise the necessary finance, minimise the risk and turn the plan into a profitable business venture.**

Some do, and some dream. Your character and skills will ultimately play the biggest part in the success of your business.

NEXT YEAR I'LL BE A MILLIONAIRE
According to one author, the successful entrepreneur should have the following characteristics:

1. Healthy (doesn't smoke or drink).
2. Dresses in smart casual clothes.

3. Wears lots of jewellery.
4. Sports a beard (so does Santa and look how busy he is).
5. Lives in an urban area.
6. 25–35 years old.
7. Excels in communication skills.
8. Drives a European car.
9. Married.
10. Heterosexual.
11. Male.

Number 4 was a dead give-away for number 11. This author has now left business school and entered the real world. Thank Heavens!

So what has suddenly changed in your life to make you consider self-employment?

◆ Uncertain job prospects?
◆ The sack?
◆ Can't get on with the boss?
◆ Can't handle the job?
◆ Personal upset in your life (emotional or physical)?
◆ Mid-life crisis?
◆ Someone you know is selling their business?
◆ Jealous of your self-employed friends?

These are all negative reasons for a complete change in your life and if they apply to you, think very hard before proceeding. For some people the move is a planned one, almost a natural progression. The obvious conclusion, therefore, is take some time, sit down and take a cold, honest look at yourself and your motives. If you can truly say 'for the most part my incentive is financial as well as job satisfaction' you are on the right road. You have cracked it. Now let's see if you are made of the right stuff.

SELF DISCIPLINE

Do you recognise the difference between takings and profit? If takings make you feel rich and successful, that you have 'arrived', beware – **failure is imminent!**

Profit is the balance you are left with after all your expenses have been paid. Plan and budget: it is the only way to keep your head out of the clouds and focused on the future.

TOTAL COMMITMENT AND HARD WORK

You don't have to be a workaholic but you do need to understand that the working day of the average civil servant bears no relation to the working day of a self-employed business person, neither does the relative stress level. On average the self-employed person works 35% longer. The plus side is that the self-employed person has no ceiling on their earnings.

YOUR HEALTH

It's easy to overlook the importance of your health. Minor ailments sometimes go unnoticed, regular check-ups get cancelled or at the best postponed. If you want your car to give optimum performance you have to have it serviced. If you want a heart attack at 45, may I suggest plenty of four-hour business lunches, no exercise, loads of stress, too much work and very little sleep; add to that smoke-filled meetings and copious amounts of alcohol. Your health is perhaps your most valuable asset – take care of it!

Get insurance because as a self-employed person you cannot claim sickness benefit or loss of earnings. Try regular exercise, healthy eating and regular medical check-ups. For women, breast screening and cervical smear testing are essential preventative measures. And most importantly, learn to deal with stress. Find an activity that helps you unwind and relax.

FAMILY
The budding entrepreneur must have the full support of their family. Without their backing you are not firing on all cylinders. Tick the questions below you can honestly answer 'yes' to.

1. Will you get help and support from your family?

2. Have you explained all the implications of using the family home as security to raise finance (if this applies to you)?

3. Have you worked out the income your family needs for basic survival?

4. Are your family members aware of a possible decrease in income and the consequent reduction in living standards?

If you have answered 'no' to any of the questions above it would be wise to review the situation.

DETERMINATION

You'll need 'true grit'. Expect an abundance of crises. Set your goals but be ready to throw them to the wind. Self employment is not for the faint hearted; forget the path of least resistance. Follow your plan but build in a degree of flexibility.

ENTHUSIASM

I am told it is contagious. If you have employees, inject them with your enthusiasm – you will be amazed at the result.

JUDGEMENT

Can you make a decision? Or do you drag your feet? Do you have the ability to sum up a situation, make a decision and stick to it? You can and should consult others, but at the end of the day, it's down to you. Don't be a fence-sitter. Make a decision. It may be the wrong one but next time you will be speaking from experience.

INTEGRITY

To me this is one of the most important ingredients. Customers must believe your word is your bond: suppliers must believe the same. How many times have you personally experienced someone cancelling an appointment, or worse, not showing up? **Do you re-order?** Of course not. Don't make the same mistake in your business; your clientele will grow if you keep your word.

ASKING FOR HELP

Don't be afraid to ask for advice. If the man in your favourite coffee shop keeps his staff and you don't, ask him how he does it. He will be flattered, you will be wiser.

SO YOU WANT TO BE YOUR OWN BOSS

Let's look at some possible reasons:

Loads of money

Take a close look at the statistics; yes there is a great deal of money to be had, but as long as you can sustain yourself and your family your efforts will not be in vain.

Job satisfaction

You are onto a winner here. Generating your own income is doubly rewarding, it increases your confidence and self-esteem.

You want to compete

No problem. There is plenty of competition out there. No matter what business you are contemplating, you will spend only one third of your time doing the work and two thirds trying to find it.

Better than unemployment

So long as you are making a rational decision, you are on the right track.

You simply want to be your own boss

Bear in mind that initially you will earn less money, work longer hours and your stress level will be higher. But, in the long run, the sky's the limit. There are not many obstacles that will stop a determined person.

THE PLUS AND MINUS OF RUNNING YOUR OWN BUSINESS

Plus

Who gets rich working for somebody else? If you are successful you decide how many weeks' holidays you take and how much money you draw. You may well become a big business. After all, big businesses are just successful small businesses.

Minus

- Harder work
- Longer hours
- Greater stress
- Less time for family life
- You are personally liable to your debtors and, in a worst case scenario, it could mean you selling your assets, including your home.

If you are not sure, take advice. Later on in the book I will tell you who you can contact and where to contact them.

②

Test Time

ARE YOU MENTALLY AND PHYSICALLY UP FOR IT?

If you have reached this chapter without throwing the book away, you have made a promising start. Some might say the correct place for this chapter is at the end but I did promise you a 'no bull', 'straight from the hip' approach. Complete the following questionnaires; the results will either encourage you to proceed or they will beg the question 'Are you the right person to go it alone in business?' Let's start with a list of reasons frequently given by those wanting to be their own boss. Tick the ones that have most influenced your decision.

1. To make loads of money.

2. Personal recognition.

3. The 'I did it my way' syndrome.

4. Sick of working for other people.

5. To control others.

6. Taking risks makes the adrenaline flow.

7. Greater control of my life.

8. To build a business for the financial stability of myself and my family.

9. To choose my own working hours.

10. To turn a hobby into a business.

11. To experience achievement.

12. To gain the admiration of others.

13. To impress.

14. To increase my self-esteem.

15. To climb the social ladder.

List any other reasons that may apply to you; your business plan will be enhanced if you are aware of your motivations. A persistent and strong personality is a trait found in all successful business people and is something to nurture and be proud of. Entrepreneurs I have interviewed show a high level of self discipline allied to a high level of concentrated energy. They are rarely known to put off an unpleasant task if it is for the good of their business. They don't use self deception to avoid meeting head-on with painful or unpalatable decisions.

THE TEST
Here are a few of the more important qualities you will require.

		yes	no
1.	Are you persistent?	☐	☐
2.	Are you capable of hard work?	☐	☐
3.	Are you able to sell yourself to others?	☐	☐
4.	Are you self motivating?	☐	☐
5.	Are you able to accept criticism?	☐	☐
6.	Are you an organised person?	☐	☐

7. Are you reliable? ☐ ☐

8. Are you able to enthuse others? ☐ ☐

If you have answered 'yes' to at least 7 out of 8, carry on. You *must* be able to answer 'yes' to *all five* of the following:

1. Are you skilled in your chosen field? ☐ ☐

2. Are you able to learn? ☐ ☐

3. Do you have a professional manner? ☐ ☐

4. Do you have patience with people around you? ☐ ☐

5. Are you healthy? ☐ ☐

Now for the big one – are you ready?

Tick any of the following that apply to you.

How good at working are you?

1. I give up easily ☐

2. If it's for me I will work hard ☐

3. Only fools and horses work ☐

How do you deal with other people?

4. Other people get on my nerves ☐

5. I make friends with everyone ☐

6. I tolerate people ☐

7. I fool people into thinking I like them ☐

Are you a leader?

8. People seem to want to help me ☐

9. If all else fails, I threaten people ☐

10. If all else fails, I bribe people ☐

11. If all else fails, I give up ☐

12. I work with others to get the job done ☐

13. I'm OK as long as somebody gets me started ☐

14. I don't respond unless I have to ☐

15. Nobody needs to tell me, I do it on my own ☐

Tenacious or not?

13. I finish what I start ☐

14. I am easily distracted ☐

15. I am like a dog with a bone ☐

16. If it doesn't go right I get bored ☐

Are you trustworthy?

17. My word is my bond ☐

18. I promise the earth ☐

19. I don't say it if I can't do it ☐

20. I believe that what they don't see can't hurt them ☐

It's decision time

21. I let others take the decisions ☐

22. Instant decisions are best ☐

23. I never change my mind ☐

24. I listen to everybody's views then formulate my decision ☐

25. I seek no-one's advice ☐

26. A wrong decision is better than no decision
    at all ☐

The purpose of the previous 26 questions was to make you aware of your strengths and weaknesses. No two people are alike and for that reason some businesses suit some people better than others. For example, a nervous, easily stressed person may wish to reconsider the idea of opening a stock broking business or driving school, and a flamboyant outgoing person may find sitting at home alone in front of a computer impossible. Quite simply then, **be honest with yourself**.

ESSENTIAL SKILLS

There are a great number of skills attached to running a business; many of them can be acquired free of charge from the numerous business support agencies (see Chapter 14).

Place a tick against those skills and knowledge areas listed below that you are lacking, but only if they are relevant to your business:

1. Ability to sell ☐
2. Knowledge of market research ☐
3. Bookkeeping ☐
4. Understanding of cash control ☐
5. Ability to raise finance ☐
7. Negotiating skills ☐
8. Knowledge of employment law ☐

9. Understanding of stock control   ☐

10. Understanding of the methods used to
    establish prices   ☐

11. Understanding of the statutory requirements
    of HM Customs and Excise, VAT and PAYE   ☐

Answering the above questions truthfully will leave you one of four roads to travel:

◆   proceed
◆   delay
◆   research and train
◆   give up.

The following chapters will, I hope, answer many of your questions and Chapter 14 will identify those organisations set up to help and advise people in your situation.

Good – now just to round off this section, one more point:

I will succeed because_____

_____

Well that's the worst over. You can relax a little now, put your feet up, read the *Financial Times*, have forty winks. If you're too excited, turn to Chapter 3.

(3)

Selecting the Right Business

Selecting the right business has many of the same elements as seeking the right career. The previous chapter helped you identify and become conscious of your strengths and weaknesses. Identifying the right business and relating those strengths and weaknesses to it must therefore be the next logical step.

Clearly a person who loves tinkering with cars will be much happier owning a garage business than a newsagent's. Reflect on your background life experiences. Brainstorm your thoughts and ideas, put them down on paper and sort your ideas into groups: possible, difficult but possible, unlikely, impossible. Don't be restricted by traditional methods. New twists can be exciting and highly successful. Remember, we live in the age of constant innovation – think about Velcro or Dyson vacuum cleaners. And we haven't even touched on computers yet.

In Chapter 9 we investigate the pros and cons of working from home. For now, in our quest to consider the right business, here are a few home possibilities. Don't forget the previous chapter should have identified if you have the self-discipline and the self-motivation to make working from home a realistic option.

There are many businesses that can be run from home:

◆ web design
◆ graphic design
◆ hairdressing
◆ bookkeeping
◆ telesales
◆ consultancy
◆ pet photography
◆ child minding
◆ architectural services
◆ chiropody
◆ homeopathy
◆ art
◆ craft design and manufacture
◆ teaching
◆ antique dealing
◆ dressmaking
◆ aromatherapy.

This list is just a sample. Jot down your own ideas: you will be amazed at the number and diversity of sound business ideas you can operate from your home. But a word of caution – the authorities can object and take action if it is creating noise or nuisance to your neighbours.

To receive more information on this subject log on to www.smallbusiness.com or contact your local Enterprise Agency – you will find them in the telephone directory or at www.yell.com Try looking at *Exchange and Mart* or publications such as *Business Ideas* to help you brainstorm entrepreneurial ideas.

SELECTING YOUR BUSINESS LOCATION

The right location for your business is essential for its success. Look closely at the type of business, the type of market and your financial restraints. Below are a few important considerations:

The purchasing patterns of your customers

Does your market research indicate the need for your business to be near similar businesses? Does your research point you towards out-of-town shopping complexes? Or perhaps you will benefit by being close to a transport terminus.

Transport

If your business is mail order, for example, will you need to be within striking distance of road, rail, air or sea?

Up-and-coming location

Be wary of areas that are beginning to look desolate – for example, those that have premises with short-term letting agreements, charity shops or empty shops. You would be wise to investigate the cause.

Image

Ensure the premises project the right image to your customers.

Unforeseen developments

Search for any information on potential changes in the immediate area of your business.

PURCHASING A BUSINESS

Buying an existing business can be a risk, especially for the first-time buyer. In my opinion, far too much emphasis is placed on the vendor's accounts. They will only give you half the story – for example, accounts don't tell you that a road is being planned which will run directly through your premises, they don't tell you that a new hypermarket is about to be constructed a few yards from your shop, selling the same goods discounted below your wholesale purchase price. Accounts tell you only financial facts from the past with no guarantee they will continue. There is no mention in the written record of customer loyalty to the vendor. An unscrupulous businessman will sell you the business and then take the customers with him to a similar venture a few yards down the road.

Despite all the above disadvantages there are some distinct advantages to buying an existing business. Less time is likely to be taken to reach profitability when you purchase a going concern, less money has to be spent attempting to make the public aware of your business location. Existing trading links such as wholesalers and manufacturers' representatives will continue, saving a great deal of time and effort trying to source them.

As a rule of thumb, use all the help you can get. This would include solicitors, accountants, local planning authorities and your local Chamber of Commerce.

Take the following points into consideration:

- Can the vendor supply three years' audited accounts?

- Investigate the true reason for the sale.

- Be sure to write an inventory of the fixtures and fittings on the first occasion you view.

- Stock at valuation following a stock-take should be paid for at the same time that the keys are handed over and not before.

- Does the existing net profit pay the bills, cover your basic survival income requirements and leave enough to allow some re-investment in the business?

- Watch out for trends. High closing stocks will push up the profit figure and push up the price.

- Set a ceiling on the price you are prepared to pay and do not exceed it.

- If you are buying stock, check its saleability and the price you are being charged.

- Calculate the time it will take to recoup the asking price.

- Shop around – check the list which follows to ensure you are getting value for money.

- Establish and investigate all commercial threats to the business.

- Rent or buy? Check out Chapter 8 of this book. What steps will you take to ensure you retain the existing clientele?

♦ Look for hidden costs, for example, faulty or non-compliant electrical fittings, non-compliant fire fighting equipment.

♦ Check for bad financial business practices on the part of the vendor. Blacklisting by suppliers can take a long time to shake off and can ruin your business before you start.

LOOKING FOR BUSINESS IDEAS
♦ Consult business transfer agents.
♦ Look in directories at your local library.
♦ Can your hobbies provide a starting point?
♦ Did you excel in any one subject at school?
♦ Are you a sportsman/woman?
♦ Find a gap in an existing market.
♦ Look for a product that requires updating.
♦ Visit your local Enterprise Agency.

WHAT ARE YOUR REQUIREMENTS?
We all have differing responsibilities, requirements and restraints, be they financial, family, health or merely age. Allow me to give an example. Jane is a single mother of two young children and has limited finance with little or no security. On the plus side, she has a clean credit record, loves children and is a hard worker. She can only work during school hours, as she cannot afford to employ a child minder. Jane studied fashion design at school, but although she had flair she was restricted by her domestic life.

Working from home would suit Jane for the following reasons:

◆ She can fit working hours around her family's needs.
◆ It minimises overheads.
◆ She gains a small tax advantage.
◆ There are no travel expenses.

She also has the following requirements:

◆ a business that does not mean employing staff – less paperwork, lower outgoings
◆ a business with a minimum investment required.

Listing your own requirements is essential in the business selection process. Divide your requirements into essential and non-essential. Your list might include some of the following:

◆ Minimum finance requirement.
◆ Minimum risk.
◆ No unsociable hours or the opposite.
◆ No travelling or the opposite.
◆ Must have expansion potential.
◆ Minimum of paperwork.
◆ Meeting people.
◆ No staff.
◆ Will not require me to move home.
◆ Minimum delay in profitability.
◆ Preferably a cash business.

INNOVATION

Spotting a gap in the market and exploiting it is not just the domain of super rich businessmen like our intrepid balloon-flying Sir Richard Branson. It isn't easy but let me throw in a few ideas.

Rising crime brings with it the opportunity for all sorts of innovative products. If you are unable to manufacture due to financial or other restraints, search for the right product to import. The list is endless.

Take note of what you hear people say, for example:

◆   'If only we had one of those shops in our area.'

◆   'I would be willing to pay a little more if the quality was better.'

◆   'More of my friends would shop here if only the shops opened later.'

NITTY GRITTY TIME

The market for your product or service is absolutely crucial. Without a market you are on the road to nowhere. Basic questions have to be asked, so here we go.

1.   What is the size of the market for your product or service?

2.   Is there room in it for you?

3.   What are the reasons your product or service is better than your competitors?

4.   What share of the market can you realistically aim for?

5.   Is it a growing or contracting market?

Try to answer as many of the following questions as you feel apply to you and your proposed business. They may well help you to identify and fill in any gaps in the plan you are formulating.

Pricing

	yes	no
1. Are your prices competitive?	☐	☐
2. Do you know how to work out your price?	☐	☐

3. What will you do if you are not making sufficient profit, but stiff competition does not allow you to increase your prices?_____

_____

_____

Purchasing

	yes	no
4. Do you know how to source your suppliers?	☐	☐
5. Do you know if you are better served with a few or many suppliers?	☐	☐
6. Do you know if your credit rating will stand up to scrutiny?	☐	☐

Equipment

	yes	no
7. Do you know what equipment you need?	☐	☐
8. Do you know where to purchase it?	☐	☐
9. New or second hand?	☐	☐

Sales

	yes	no
10. Have you had any sales training experience?	☐	☐

11. Have you ascertained your customers' needs? ☐ ☐

12. Do you know how to present your merchandise/service? ☐ ☐

13. Do you know the best method of getting your message to your potential customers? ☐ ☐

Systems

14. Do you have an accountant? ☐ ☐

15. Do you have a solicitor? ☐ ☐

16. Do you require any permits to run your business? ☐ ☐

17. Do you require planning permission for a change of use for the proposed business premises? ☐ ☐

18. Do you need to register for VAT? ☐ ☐

The importance of marketing

Let us suppose you have designed a new type of shovel. Be sure the people want it, be sure you can manufacture it, be sure you are in the right place to sell it and be sure you can deliver it. Knowing the people are out there just isn't good enough. Be sure to cost the product out to the last penny and remember:

Any fool can work for nothing.

The Business Plan

The previous chapters have in the main been devoted to assessing and evaluating the strengths and weaknesses of your business idea as well as your own characteristics, motives and abilities. Now it's time to get the whole shooting match down on paper. A format for a business plan can easily be acquired from any of the high street banks, from your local Enterprise Agency or from www.smallbusiness.com However, you may wish to write your business plan using your own format.

Producing a business plan is no guarantee that a business will be a success but it does serve to present and formalise your ideas and abilities. Visit the bank you are proposing to approach and pick up a copy of their business start-up literature and software. It will lead you through the business plan step by step. Alternatively you could make an appointment with a business advisor at your local Enterprise Agency; and here's the good news, **it's all free of charge**.

Why is it then that so many entrepreneurs attempt to start their business without a plan? There are two reasons often given:

1. I am not giving away my ideas and financial information.

2. I am funding it myself, I do not need to borrow money.

BENEFITS OF A BUSINESS PLAN

1. A mistake made and recognised on paper is much better than a mistake made when your business is up and running.

2. A business plan will focus your mind on the targets, forecasts and realities of business problems and hurdles.

3. Raising finance will undoubtedly necessitate a business plan and a cash flow forecast.

4. A business plan will make you aware of the many facets of self-employment and will enable you to understand and react more quickly to problems.

As well as the above, think of your business plan as an advertising leaflet, or to put it another way, a piece of literature designed to sell you and your business idea. Any interested party who needs convincing will insist on seeing your business plan. The list may include:

- the bank manager
- a potential sponsor
- the Prince's Business Trust
- a business investment partner
- a commercial property landlord.

WRITING YOUR PLAN

The plan needs to show:

1. That you are capable of business success.

2. That you have done your homework (product testing, marketing, competition, etc.).

3. That you are realistic in your approach.

4. That you know the best route to reach your goal.

Type your plan on a word-processor – don't hand-write it. Bear the following points in mind:

1. Hit the reader with an attention-grabbing statement, e.g. 'This low-priced product has features found only in the competition's high price range'.

2. Keep it short. Generally speaking, the reader will be a busy person, and keeping it short will retain their interest.

3. Always be precise and explicit with your plan. Don't forget the reader may not understand jargon and abbreviations associated with your chosen sector of business.

4. Don't waffle. (No need to pad it out with irrelevancies, e.g. 'The intention is to paint the staff toilet blue, complementing that with yellow light fittings'.)

5. Include your CV, linking your experience to your proposed business.

A business plan consists of:

- content
- focus
- presentation and layout
- oral presentation.

The business
1. History
2. Objectives
3. Current finance.

The service or product
1. Why you think you can sell it.
2. What makes it different to other services/products?
3. Can the market accommodate you?
4. How your experience is relevant.
5. The premises required to market or produce the service or product.

Your own strategy
1. To hit your business targets.
2. To achieve results in the market place.
3. To ensure the public are aware of your service/ product.
4. To ensure ease of accessibility to your service/ product.
5. To capitalise on the failings of your product/service competition.

Let's assume you are planning to turn your hobby, designing and making pottery, into a business. Study and assess carefully factors within and outside your plan.

OUTSIDE FACTORS

Political
Is election time nearing? Could a change of government affect your business? E.g.:

◆   A change in advertising practices.

◆   A change in trading hours.

◆   A change in packaging or labelling legislation.

◆   New plans for housing.

Economic
◆   Perhaps a change in VAT, import or export duty is imminent.

◆   Does recession increase or decrease your business?

◆   What grants or subsidies are available? (Contact your local enterprise agency.)

◆   Check the latest figures relating to disposable income. (Contact the Department of Trade and Industry listed in Chapter 14.)

◆   How does inflation affect your business? Can the increases be passed on to your customers or will it trigger a price war with your competitors?

Social
◆   Check the unemployment figures in your client groups.

◆   Population changes, e.g. racial, religious and the percentage of young to old, may also need to be investigated.

◆　Environmental issues can also affect your business.

Technological

◆　Does your proposed business make full use of technological changes, or are you giving your competitors an edge?

◆　Are you able to read the signs leading up to technological changes?

◆　Have you investigated the pattern of change over the last five years and noted the resultant effect on the type of business you have chosen to enter?

◆　Are you able to invest in technological change at the same rate as your competitors?

Fashion changes

◆　Remember that fashions change; what's in today might be out tomorrow.

INSIDE FACTORS

Weak points

◆　Do you lack a particular skill (e.g. marketing)?
◆　What are your financial weak points?
◆　What about technology?
◆　Is geographical location a weakness?

Strengths

◆　Your own ability to design and manufacture your pottery makes you less reliant on others. Previous samples and designs will allow you to test the market.

As no two items you manufacture are the same, you can truly claim to be producing a unique product – a big sales plus.

Opportunities

♦ A local potter may recently have vacated a premises just the right location and size for you to start up your business.

Threats

♦ You may have to move fast to stop your competitors from taking advantage of the new situation.

THE DETAILS

Here are the elements you will require to complete your business plan:

1. An introduction.
2. Personal details.
3. Business description.
4. Premises.
5. Product/service description.
6. Funding details.
7. The market.
8. Competition product/service comparison chart.
9. Pricing and break even point calculation.
10. Promotion and marketing plan.
11. Bookkeeping (myself/bookkeeper/accountant).

PRICING

Before attempting to complete a cash flow forecast, you need to establish the price your customers will pay. At that point, compare your price with your competitors' price and if the cap fits wear it. A word of warning: never compete on price alone, be sure your product/service is better.

Calculating your break even point

1. Personal drawings . . . .
2. Salaries/wages . . . .
3. Tax . . . .
4. National Insurance . . . .
5. Advertising/sales promotion . . . .
6. Stationery/postage/printing . . . .
7. Rent . . . .
8. Rates . . . .
9. Water . . . .
10. Telephone . . . .
11. Fuel . . . .
12. Vehicle depreciation . . . .
13. Vehicle maintenance . . . .
14. Road tax . . . .
15. Vehicle insurance . . . .
16. Business insurance . . . .
17. Equipment depreciation . . . .
18. Bad debts . . . .
19. Bank loan . . . .
20. Bank charges . . . .
21. Solicitor/accountant fees . . . .

Total

My charge to the customer will be £ . . . . per day/per item/per hour(please delete as appropriate)

My break even point is £ . . . .

Taking into account the above calculations and before the final price is arrived at, there are a couple of other pricing influences that should be considered:

1. The safety record of the product.
2. The reliability record of the product.
3. Supply and demand for the product.
4. Promotional activity by your competition.

The price of your product or service cannot be calculated in isolation, you must consider it as part of the sales and marketing strategy, explained in more detail in Chapter 10.

CASH FLOW FORECAST

For many people preparing a cash flow forecast is a daunting task, but it doesn't have to be. When completed, your cash flow forecast will show you the actual movement of cash in and out of your business. A cash flow forecast should be drawn up for a year's trading, with a space for each month's actual figure beside the forecast figure. Drawn up properly, a cash flow forecast will give an up-to-date position at all times, invaluable when you are required to make an unexpected decision. A word of caution: bank statements do not always give you the true position. A balance will not show uncleared cheques or regular payments awaiting deduction.

Figure 1 is an example of a cash flow forecast.

	April £	May £	June £	July £	Aug £	Sept £	Oct £	Nov £	Dec £	Jan £	Feb £	March £	TOTAL £
RECEIPTS													
Invoiced Sales	16,167	16,167	16,167	16,167	16,167	16,167	16,167	16,167	16,167	16,167	16,167	16,167	194,004
Capital Introduced	100,000	–	–	–	–	–	–	–	–	–	–	–	100,000
Loan Capital	225,000	–	–	–	–	–	–	–	–	–	–	–	225,000
	341,167	16,167	16,167	16,167	16,167	16,167	16,167	16,167	16,167	16,167	16,167	16,167	519,004
PAYMENTS													
Running Costs	11,402	11,402	11,652	10,652	10,752	11,652	10,652	10,752	11,652	10,652	10,752	11,652	133,624
Loan Payments		2,216	2,215	2,216	2,216	2,215	2,216	2,216	2,215	2,216	2,216	2,215	24,372
Freehold Property	245,000	–	–	–	–	–	–	–	–	–	–	–	245,000
Goodwill	30,000	–	–	–	–	–	–	–	–	–	–	–	30,000
Fixtures & Fittings	50,000	–	–	–	–	–	–	–	–	–	–	–	50,000
	336,402	13,618	13,867	12,868	12,968	13,867	12,868	12,968	13,867	12,868	12,968	13,867	482,996
NET CASH FLOW	4,765	2,549	2,300	3,299	3,199	2,300	3,299	3,199	2,300	3,299	3,199	2,300	36,008
OPENING BANK	–	4,765	7,314	9,614	12,913	16,112	18,412	21,711	24,910	27,210	30,509	33,708	–
CLOSING BANK	4,765	7,314	9,614	12,913	16,112	18,412	21,711	24,910	27,210	30,509	33,708	36,008	36,008

Figure 1. Cash flow forecast.

The cash flow forecast is designed to predict the movement of money over the life of the forecast and, in this case, you will see that invoiced sales are received as and when invoiced and therefore there are no credit terms to customers. In some cash flow forecasts, you may find that there is a time difference between the raising of an invoice and the receipt of money, thus creating the situation where debtors will arise.

The loan capital column under receipts represents external funding.

Payments shows the payment of monies out of the business with the running costs representing the actual payment of the expenses recognised within the overheads section of the profit and loss forecast. In this case, you will see that timing differences arise throughout the year in the initial months but that the total of the overhead expenses on the profit and loss account represents the total paid out in running costs on the cash flow forecast. This is a coincidence.

The net cash flow column on the forecast represents the net movement in the month in question.

PROFIT AND LOSS FORECAST

The profit and loss forecast will summarise the sales and costs anticipated monthly over the next year. In the example opposite you may find that not all the headings are relevant to your business.

Sales

This relates to the amount of cash (in this instance, cash

	April	May	June	July	Aug	Sept	Oct	Nov	Dec	Jan	Feb	March	TOTAL
	£	£	£	£	£	£	£	£	£	£	£	£	£
INCOME													
Income	16,167	16,167	16,167	16,167	16,167	16,167	16,167	16,167	16,167	16,167	16,167	16,167	194,004
	16,167	**16,167**	**16,167**	**16,167**	**16,167**	**16,167**	**16,167**	**16,167**	**16,167**	**16,167**	**16,167**	**16,167**	**194,004**
CAPITAL INTRODUCED													
Capital Introduced	100,000												100,000
	100,000												**100,000**
GROSS PROFIT	116,167	16,167	16,167	16,167	16,167	16,167	16,167	16,167	16,167	16,167	16,167	16,167	294,004
OVERHEADS													
Wages and Salaries	8,917	8,917	8,917	8,917	8,917	8,917	8,917	8,917	8,917	8,917	8,917	8,917	107,004
Provisions	950	950	950	950	950	950	950	950	950	950	950	950	11,400
Heating & Lighting			750			750			750			750	3,000
Repairs & Renewals	250	250	250	250	250	250	250	250	250	250	250	250	3,000
Insurance	750												750
Telephone			250			250			250			250	1,000
Stationery & Advertising	40	40	40	40	40	40	40	40	40	40	40	40	480
Accountancy	750			100			100			100			1,050
Transport	100	100	100	100	100	100	100	100	100	100	100	100	1,200
Cleaning Materials	125	125	125	125	125	125	125	125	125	125	125	125	1,500
Residents' Welfare	20	20	20	20	20	20	20	20	20	20	20	20	240
Water & Environmental Charges	125	125	125	125	125	125	125	125	125	125	125	125	1,500
Sundries	125	125	125	125	125	125	125	125	125	125	125	125	1,500
	12,152	**10,652**	**11,652**	**10,752**	**10,652**	**11,652**	**10,752**	**10,652**	**11,652**	**10,752**	**10,652**	**11,652**	**133,624**
OTHER COSTS													
Depreciation	625	625	625	625	625	625	625	625	625	625	625	625	7,500
	625	**625**	**625**	**625**	**625**	**625**	**625**	**625**	**625**	**625**	**625**	**625**	**7,500**
OPERATING PROFIT	103,390	4,890	3,890	4,790	4,890	3,890	4,790	4,890	3,890	4,790	4,890	3,890	152,880
INTEREST EXPENSE													
Loan Interest		1,594	1,589	1,585	1,580	1,576	1,572	1,567	1,562	1,558	1,552	1,549	17,284
		1,594	**1,589**	**1,585**	**1,580**	**1,576**	**1,572**	**1,567**	**1,562**	**1,558**	**1,552**	**1,549**	**17,284**
NET PROFIT	**103,390**	**3,296**	**2,301**	**3,205**	**3,310**	**2,314**	**3,218**	**3,323**	**2,328**	**3,232**	**3,338**	**2,341**	**135,596**
CUMULATIVE	**103,390**	**106,686**	**108,987**	**112,192**	**115,502**	**117,816**	**121,034**	**124,357**	**126,685**	**129,917**	**133,255**	**135,596**	**135,596**

Figure 2. Profit and loss forecast

includes cheques and credit card transactions) forecast for the period less VAT, plus money owed to you at the end of the period, less the money owed at the end of the previous period, and taking into account seasonal trading variations. When calculating a sales forecast you need to consider the unit quantity you can sell and the selling price of those units.

The profit and loss forecast is designed to determine profitability on a month-by-month basis for the twelve-month period ending 31 March.

Income represents the sales made during the months, net of VAT.

Capital introduced is monies introduced from proprietors as original funding.

Overheads – this section shows the expenses of the business, by category, on a month-by-month basis as incurred.

Depreciation represents the writing down of assets over the lifetime of those assets.

Loan interest represents the interest on loans received from external funding.

The **net profit** column represents the total sums available for the proprietor to draw upon over the course of the year and shows the viability of the business. Of course, £100,000 of the profit is in actual fact the capital introduced and therefore should be disregarded from months April and the Total column.

Cost of sales (purchases)

This relates to the price you pay for the goods. If you are VAT registered you exclude VAT in your cost of sales calculation, if you are not VAT registered you include it. You will require the total of the invoices anticipated during the period. Another method, as with the sales calculation, is to take the purchase figure for the period plus money you owe to suppliers at the end of the period, less the money you owed to suppliers at the beginning of the period. When making the purchase estimate try to realistically take into account any increase in the cost of your raw materials or purchases.

Cost of sales (labour)

When making this forecast all the employer's costs such as gross salary and national insurance contributions must be included.

Cost of sales (other)

This includes all other foreseeable direct costs.

Overheads (rent and rates)

Rent – calculate the rent for each period.
Rates – break the annual figure down into equal amounts.

Overheads (heat/light)

Estimate the cost for each period.

Overheads (telephone)

Estimate the cost for each period.

Overheads (professional fees)
Enter all professional fees within the period, plus those fees not billed until the next period.

Overheads (depreciation)
Calculate the asset depreciation figure for the period by taking the capital cost of your equipment (for example, computers, cars, office furniture) – divide it by four and enter that figure in your calculation.

$$5$$

The Business Structure

TRADING METHODS

The object of this book is to guide the start-up business through the preliminary stages – that is, from idea to reality. No one publication can cover all aspects of business. For this reason I have chosen to concentrate on the first four out of the six listed below recognised as the legal trading methods in the United Kingdom; these are the most likely choice for the start-up business:

1. Sole trader.
2. Partnership.
3. Limited company.
4. Franchise.
5. Registered charity.
6. Multi-level marketing.

SOLE TRADER

It is not necessary for sole traders to register their trading name with any government or official body. It is, however, required of the sole trader to inform the Inland Revenue and the Contributions Agency. If the real or anticipated annual turnover is at the current VAT threshold level or above you will need to register for VAT (see Chapter 7). The only other obligations require you to print your name and the name of the business on any stationery. While we are on the subject of names, using your own name, e.g.

Paul Hayes Builder, does not require you to check for duplication, but a name that is not yours, such as Disney Builders, may well meet with objections. If in doubt **check it out** (take professional advice).

The sole trader is not required to have audited accounts. However, finance permitting, an accountant is a good investment.

Advantages
1. You can start trading immediately.

2. No start-up costs.

3. Reduced professional fees.

4. You can offset some business expenses against earnings for tax purposes.

5. Flexibility – considerably less restriction from official bodies.

6. Your affairs remain private and cannot be exposed to the public.

7. You pay tax as a self-employed person (Schedule D).

8. Your profit and loss, in one trade, can be set against any other earned income in the year, or against past PAYE in certain cases.

9. You will truly be master of your own destiny.

Disadvantages
1. Responsibility starts and ends with you. Bankruptcy allows your creditors to seize and sell not only your business but your personal possessions as well: your

home, and your car.

2. In the business pecking order the sole trader takes up the rear.

3. The sole trader cannot use equity capital, only finance provided by banks or individuals and non-equity sources.

4. The business dies with you.

The buck starts and stops with you.

PARTNERSHIP

It would be quite wrong of me to quote my own bad partnership experiences; suffice it to say that the only business partnership that has been successful for me in my 44 years of self-employment is the one I now have with my wife.

Just as for the sole trader the only requirements are:

1. Show clearly the names and address of your business on all stationery.

2. Be sure there are no objections to your chosen business name.

3. Check the current registration threshold with your local VAT office.

Partnership can lead to problems and here's why:

1. Friendship is the most common reason for going into

a business partnership – but is your friend a good business person?

2. Personality conflicts might damage the business.

3. Outside influences such as husbands/wives may demonstrate personal likes and dislikes.

4. There might be dishonesty or irresponsibility on the part of one partner or the other.

5. You might have conflicting goals.

6. The balance of work and duties might not be fairly distributed.

7. There might be a lack of meaningful communication.

8. Bankruptcy of a partner does not make you liable for their debt, but it can cause you serious financial problems if you try to purchase the share of the business that is in the hands of the receiver or the creditors.

The Partnership Act

1. Partners must share profit and loss at an agreed percentage level.

2. Partners must share capital investment at an agreed percentage level.

3. There will be no interest paid on capital introduced by any partner, unless it is paid at an agreed percentage level.

4. Partners must have a say in the running of the business at an agreed percentage level.

5. Partners cannot draw a salary (salary can be drawn

from their capital account, e.g. with accountants' and solicitors' practices).

6. Time off and the frequency of holidays should be determined and laid down in advance.

7. All partners have voting rights.

This is by no means a complete list. Ask your solicitor for a copy of a Deed of Partnership. You may wish to alter the clauses which you are quite entitled to alter. Any contract should cover the following points:

1. Voting rights and policy decisions.

2. Profit sharing, responsibilities and duration.

3. Withdrawing capital.

4. Time off.

5. Accounting system.

Limited partnership
Known affectionately as a sleeping partner, they can play no active part in the management of the business and they are excluded from writing cheques on the business account or signing contracts. By registering a limited partnership, sleeping partners can protect themselves against the debt or obligations of their partners.

Partnership selection
Trust, and the ability to work in harmony, are the main ingredients necessary for a successful partnership. Search your motives: are you really the type of person who is

capable of listening to another person's point of view, or are you a control freak? Partnership is almost like marriage; be sure to take lots of time in choosing your partner, because divorce and partnership break up are not only expensive but emotionally exhausting as well.

Advantages
1. No audit required.
2. Trading information does not need to be made public.
3. You pay tax on a self-employed basis (Schedule D).

Disadvantages
1. You and your partners are jointly and personally liable for all of the business debts.
2. Partnerships are generally dissolved on the death of a partner.
3. Partnership contracts are expensive.
4. You will have limited borrowing facilities (often dependent on the individual partners' financial position).

LIMITED COMPANIES
A limited company must obey the rules laid down in company law; that is, they must maintain accounts. Over £1 million annual turnover requires them to have an annual audit and they must be prepared to disclose the company's activities to the general public. The owner or owners of the company are the shareholders, liable for all the debts to the face value of their shares. Many lending

institutions will now request personal guarantees from a director. Trading while knowing that the company is insolvent can lead to criminal prosecution.

A minimum of two shareholders and one director are required to form a limited company in accordance with the Companies Act. There are two types of company limited by shares:

1. **A private company.** Most companies start life this way and it is not until substantial funds are required from shareholders that they go public.

2. **A public company (PLC)** which has a minimum allotted share capital of £50,000.00 can be quoted on the Stock Exchange and the public are able to purchase shares.

All limited companies pay Corporation Tax on their taxable profits.

To register as a limited company you are required to submit a Memorandum of Association to Companies House (Cardiff for England and Wales, Edinburgh for Scotland, and Belfast for Northern Ireland). The following must be included in the Memorandum (it is advisable to seek professional help to register):

1. The company name.

2. Country of registration.

3. Share capital total and division.

4. A clear statement of the limited liability of the members.

5. The object of the company.

6. It must be signed and witnessed.

Next the Articles of Association must be submitted. Any deviation from the standard articles under the Companies Act must also be submitted. Other forms to register are:

♦   first directors
♦   secretary details
♦   consent to act
♦   the registered office
♦   address of the company
♦   the statutory declaration that all the formalities have been complied with.

The current cost of all this is £20 for a new registration, £10 for a change of company name, and £15 per annum for filing the company's annual return with the registrar of companies.

Advantages

1. The image projected is high status.

2. Equity capital can be raised.

3. Limited liability (liability to the value of the shares only).

Disadvantages

1. Banks and suppliers will often insist on personal guarantees.

2. Certificate of Incorporation required before you trade.

3. Directors are on PAYE.

4. Over £1 million turnover will involve a full accounting audit.

FRANCHISE

Definition

Franchising is an innovative marketing technique for the improvement and expansion of products and services distribution.

History

A number of factors have been involved in the success of franchising. During the 1980s, recession created an unusual situation; people were being made redundant from their jobs and in many cases given large redundancy payments. Being too old or overqualified were just some of the reasons why those people found it difficult to get further employment. To start their own business was considered too risky, they only had the one sum of money so they had to minimise the risk. Franchising was the answer, a tried and tested formula was the safest bet. The government's recognition of the importance of small businesses and the rapid growth of the fast food industry were also major contributions to the success of franchising.

How does it work?

The principle of franchising is that a successful company wishing to extend its field of trading sells you, the franchisee, the right to use its name, experience and reputation. There are no hard and fast rules; the diversity of business makes that impossible. There are two basic types:

1. retail and catering

2. services, such as drain cleaning, carpet, furniture and house cleaning and car repairs.

Big name franchises can open doors, for example the banks are more likely to listen to a tried and tested formula. Sometimes the franchisor will lease or mortgage the property to you, but there are always systems that limit the way in which you are able to trade.

The British Franchising Association has produced a guide, *An Introduction to Franchising* (URN 96/999), which can be obtained from the DTI Small Firms Publications, Admail 528, London SW1W 8YT. Tel: 020 7510 0169, fax: 020 7510 0197.

An important fact to keep in mind when considering the purchase of a franchise is that, if the parent company is a successful household name such as Wimpy or Kentucky Fried Chicken, there will be a number of applicants and the purchase price is likely to be high. The franchisor will require references from you and you will require details of pilot schemes run by the franchisor.

The contract
Professional advice is advisable throughout the negotiations and in particular at the contract stage. Your legal advisor will scrutinise the contract and highlight areas of risk or clauses that require clarification. Your accountant will check the figures and may even come across costs to you that are negotiable.

Main points of the contract
1. The cost of the total franchise package.

2. The length of time the franchise will run.

3. The type of business and operating conditions.

4. The franchise operation address.

5. The franchisee's rights to sell the franchise.

6. Contract termination by the franchisee or the franchisor.

A franchise is a fashionable way to start in business and reduce the risk. However, there are pros and cons:

Advantages
1. You are trading under the umbrella of a household name.

2. You will benefit from local and national advertising.

3. Training is given in all aspects of running your franchise correctly.

Disadvantages
1. There is always a franchise fee.

2. There are always start-up costs, often quite large.

3. There are management fees throughout the length of
    the contract – the norm is around 10%.

6

Raising Finance

BANKS

Believe it or not, banks do actually want to lend you
money but, just as you would, they want to be as sure as
possible that they will get the money back. In short, they
want to be sure that your business is one they want to be
involved with.

Insurance policies, pensions and investments are all part
of a bank's business, but make no mistake, their prime
objective is to sell money, to make money. The bank
manager's job is to ensure the operation runs smoothly.
So he or she is there to sell money, you are there to buy
money. **You are the customer**. Compare their terms with
others and if you are not comfortable with the individual
you are dealing with, visit another bank. In the world of
banking there are horses for courses, in other words
different banks in different areas view things in different
ways. For example, a business dealing with fashion or
photographic models stands a better chance of a London
bank understanding the risks involved than a country
town bank. Alternatively, a loan application for the
purchase of farm equipment stands a greater chance of
success with a rural area bank.

The accepted method of making a funding request is by
way of the business plan (refer to Chapter 4). The cash

flow forecast will give a very good indication of the level of funding, the length of pay back time and when it is required.

Start by making an appointment with the manager to discuss your financial requirements. You will soon gauge the reaction, which may range from a definite 'no' to a 'maybe' to a 'yes', but try to prepare your answers to the manager's probing questions in advance.

Never forget the reason that many loan applications fail; it is because they are badly presented. A 'maybe' or a 'yes' means you should return armed with a business plan and a cash flow forecast and be ready to give detailed answers to some vital questions. If you have an accountant at this stage in your business set up, ask him to attend the bank with you and if all goes to plan, ask for the maximum pay-back period. You can always clear the loan prematurely if your business takes off.

Amount required

Step number one has to be the question, 'what is the total finance required to start your business?'

What is the money for?

Clearly identify your requirements. Is it fixed capital – that is, money tied up in property, equipment and vehicles – or is it working capital, that is, money to purchase stock and for general day-to-day running costs?

How will you repay the loan and over what period?

Show clearly the amount and the method of repayment and how that relates to your cash flow forecast and business plan.

What collateral or assurance can you give that your bank will get their money back?

Demonstrate by using your cash flow forecast and your business plan your ability to repay the loan you are applying for.

What kind of financial shape are you in personally?

List all your personal outgoings: rent, food, clothing, etc. The total will be shown as personal drawings on your cash flow forecast. In most cases the lender will be looking for you to commit a minimum of one third of the required amount as a sign of good faith.

What security is available?

The lender may ask if you are prepared to have a charge placed on any freehold property owned by you. In some cases a charge on a long lease in your possession will be acceptable.

FUNDING OPTIONS

1. Personal savings
2. Bank
3. Building society
4. Merchant bank
5. Insurance companies

6. Mortgage top up
7. Grants.

The Prince's Business Trust is a trust set up and headed by Prince Charles to offer advice and, in some cases, funding to unemployed people aged between 18 and 29 inclusive. It can provide:

◆ loans of up to £5,000

◆ grants of up to £1,500 per person or £3,000 if the business involves two or more people

◆ grants for market research of up to £250 per business.

Business development scheme
Loans are available, repayable up to 20 years, for business growth (contact Business Link or your local Enterprise Agency).

Loan guarantee scheme
Financial help is offered to businesses with a viable business plan but which lack track record or security. The government backed scheme guarantees up to a maximum of 85% of loans over a two- to ten-year period, in return for a premium on the guaranteed portion of the loan. A business that is under two years old is classified as a new business and has a loan limit of £100,000. Retail industries are not included in this scheme.

Finance companies
Finance companies are generally considered to be a last resort for the borrower due to the higher rate of interest

charged. The reason for the higher rate is that the finance companies are borrowing the money themselves, so the charges they have to pay need to be met as well as their charges to you.

Overdraft facility

Often overlooked in business start-up books, the humble overdraft is a must for accounts that swing in and out of credit. In effect, it is a very short-term loan that can temporarily ease your cash flow problems.

Leasing

Great care must be exercised when considering leasing. The best advice is to take advice; the small print can cause you problems in the future. One of the advantages of leasing is that expensive items such as an ice-cream machine or a dishwasher, costing many thousands of pounds, can be acquired without paying a hefty deposit. Leasing also leaves your capital free for other use.

Hire purchase

This enables you to spread the payment over a period of one to five years. In most cases the rate of interest the dealer charges is higher than the banks, although the trend now is to offer a shorter payback period with no interest charge.

REDUCING YOUR BORROWING REQUIREMENTS

In the event of an initial refusal to your request for finance, here are a few ways to reduce your requirements:

Stock

1. Are better, more frequent deliveries an option?
2. Is a longer credit facility possible?
3. Are your stock levels too high?

Running costs

1. Is self-employed labour an option?
2. Can you pay your basic overheads over a longer period?
3. Can you link pay to productivity?

Equipment

Can you reduce your borrowing requirements by leasing or renting high-price items of equipment, technology or machinery? The simple answer is 'yes'. You will reduce your borrowing requirements but you will increase your weekly/monthly outgoings.

Debtors

1. Can you afford them?
2. Can you reduce the number of days' credit?
3. Can you turn an account customer into a cash customer?

MAKING PROVISION FOR BAD DEBT

Unfortunately bad debt is a fact of business life. An efficient day-to-day accounting system will flag up late payments. You can then refuse to provide further goods or services until the outstanding debt is paid. Many small businesses have ended in bankruptcy because they were financially unable to continue to give extended credit periods, often to companies much bigger than them. If it is at all possible try to protect yourself by setting aside a special fund or by insurance (generally only available for business-to-business bad debt protection).

(7)

Bookkeeping

WHY BOTHER?

Considered by most people in business to be a necessary evil, bookkeeping can be as difficult or as easy as you wish to make it. Rule 1: get yourself a workable system, stick with it and, most of all, stay on top of the workload. It is not uncommon for the owner of a bankrupt business to claim they did not know what was happening until it was too late. Even the most modest of accounting systems will tell you the important facts, at the same time complying with the tax authorities' requirements. Always remember your business accounts and records can be investigated by the Inland Revenue; this can be on a purely random basis or when there is reason to believe an understating of profits has occurred. Information extracted from your books will be crucial when agreeing or disputing tax demands. Other advantages are help with making cash flow forecasts and important business decisions.

Listed below are just some of the questions good bookkeeping can help you answer:

1. How much profit am I making?
2. How much do I owe?
3. How much am I owed?
4. What is my current cash position?
5. When is the right time to purchase new equipment?

6. What is the business worth in fixed and current assets?

RECEIPTS AND PAYMENTS

A complex system is unnecessary for the small business; a simple dated 'cash in' and 'cash out' record as shown below will suffice.

Receipts	Payments
Date_____ Amount_____	Date_____ Amount_____
Description_____	Description_____

In practice, it would be useful to be able to analyse further both receipts and payments under their segregated headings, e.g. a payment made for office cleaning would be under a different heading to a payment made to a supplier of raw materials. A visit to your accountant will doubtless tell you the best system for both you and your accountant, bearing in mind your accountant has to decipher your books at the end of the year so that he or she can satisfy the Inland Revenue on your behalf.

A typical breakdown is as follows:

1. Materials
2. Capital equipment
3. Travel/fuel
4. Light/heat
5. Printing and stationery
6. Advertising
7. Insurance

8. Telephone
9. Postage
10. Petty cash
11. Drawings for personal use

This list is an example and is by no means exhaustive.

OFF-THE-SHELF SYSTEMS

Most good stationers will supply you with a complete bookkeeping system ranging in price from around £200 down to £30. All have instructions and you can adjust and modify them to your requirements. **Speak to your accountant.** Computer bookkeeping systems are dealt with in Chapter 8.

PETTY CASH

Petty cash is a small amount of cash used to pay everyday minor bills such as milk, sugar, window cleaner, etc. It is usual for the cash to be kept in a box or tin and recorded in the Petty Cash Book. Once a week these figures are transferred to your accounts books and the money replaced in your tin. At the same time it is advisable to check that the amount replaced plus the amount in the tin total the petty cash allowance and the Petty Cash Book is clearly underlined ready to start again. When transferring the record of petty cash expenditure to your main accounts book, enter the total figure of each transaction into the total cash column, enter the VAT in the special VAT column and the net figure in the analysis column (see Figure 3).

OUTGOINGS

WEEK COMMENCING:- 01.01.05

DATE	CHQ NO.	AMOUNT	DATE	PAYEE	TOTAL CASH	VAT	REPAIRS	STATIONERY	PURCHASES	SUNDRY
01.01.05	111222	£100.00	02/01/05	POST OFFICE	£3.24			£3.24		
			04/01/05	TESCO STORES	£1.50				£1.50	
			01/05/05	B&M DIY STORE	£27.99	£4.17	£23.82			
			01/06/05	W H SMITH	£6.27	£0.93		£5.34		
				TOTALS	£39.00	£5.10	£23.82	£8.58	£1.50	
				(£100 - £39.00 = petty cash balance of £61.00. Cheque drawn for £39.00 bringing balance to £100.)						
08.05.05	111223	£39.00								

WEEK COMMENCING 08.05.05

OPENING BALANCE | £100.00

Figure 3. Petty cash record.

Beware of receiving a receipt for small purchases that has no VAT number printed on it Don't be afraid to ask for a written receipt no matter how small the amount, you cannot claim your VAT back without a VAT registration number. **It's your money.**

WAGES

As soon as you employ staff in your business you are required to keep a Wages Book and employee records. It is also necessary to record personal details, such as:

- Name
- Address
- Date of birth
- Date work with you commenced
- Salary
- National Insurance number
- Position held
- Date of job cessation.

In order to keep your paperwork tidy, allocate a file for each employee. That file will contain job application forms, references, contract of employment and all other relevant information. They should be kept securely locked away; remember that they are private and confidential.

The Inspector of Taxes will send you the appropriate forms to record your employees' deductions as well as the information package you will require explaining the system of wage deductions and the methods you may use to remit those deductions to the collector of taxes.

MONTH ENDING 04/10/04

NAME	TAX CODE	NATIONAL INS. NUMBER	N TABLE LETTER	GROSS AMOUNT DUE	TAX	CLASS 1	NET AMOUNT DUE	EMPLOYER'S CONTRIBUTION		
								EMPLOYER'S CONTRIBUTION		
A GREEN	438L	YP 201110C	A	£1,500.00	£236.92	£117.20	£1,145.88	£138.59		

Figure 4. Sample wages book entry.

A record of employees' absence due to illness is needed to calculate their statutory sick pay. Once again the inspector will furnish the explanatory booklets. Your employees must receive a payslip detailing the make-up and deductions affecting their salary and you will keep a summary of the information in a Wage Book (see Figure 4).

If training is needed in maintaining PAYE records, the Inland Revenue Business Support Team will be happy to train yourself and your staff.

VALUE ADDED TAX OR VAT

VAT – the very letters send shivers down the backs of many budding entrepreneurs but with no real justification. For most small businesses, assuming your books are kept up to date, VAT is a piece of cake.

The do's and don'ts

1. If your turnover in any twelve month period is likely to exceed the VAT registration threshold **you must register for VAT.**

2. Exempt businesses such as property investment, banking and insurance services cannot recover VAT that they have paid.

3. Ignorance of the VAT threshold is no excuse, the VAT office will still demand payment even if it has not been charged by you to your customer.

4. You are required to keep proof of all your inputs and outputs.

5.   Attempts to defraud VAT can lead to a spell in prison. **Beware!** Customs and Excise have the power to enter and search your premises.

6.   The VAT return form, along with any payment due, must reach HM Customs and Excise by the date shown on the return. Failure to comply will incur a penalty.

7.   There are benefits. VAT can be reclaimed on capital items, a big plus for the new business.

The VAT office has an excellent support team who give talks and guidance in seminars and training sessions across the country, or just phone and they will send you their easy-to-follow starter's guide. HM Customs and Excise head office is based at Southend-on-Sea, the final destination for your VAT return form and your payment. Under Customs and Excise in the phonebook you will find the number of your local office. The many books and leaflets that describe the various aspects can be found there. Below are some useful tips:

♦   VAT must be accounted for each time you make a taxable supply, that constitutes your output, and the VAT is your output tax.

♦   The registered person can be a sole trader, a partnership, a limited company, a club, an association or a charity.

♦   A registration embraces all the business activities of the registered entity. **Remember** that for sole traders it is the person and not the business that is registered.

SAMPLE VAT RETURN FORM

		£	p
VAT due in this period on sales and other outputs	1	3830	29
VAT due in this period on acquisitions from other EC Member states	2		
Total VAT due (the sum of boxes 1 and 2)	3	3830	29
VAT reclaimed in this period on purchases and other inputs (including acquisitions from the EC)	4	1769	57
Net VAT to be paid to Customs or reclaimed by you (Difference between boxes 3 and 4)	5	2060	72
Total value of sales and all other outputs excluding any VAT. Include your box 8 figure	6	21985	00
Total value of purchases and all others inputs excluding any VAT. Include your box 9 figure	7	15717	00
Total value of all supplies of goods and related services, excluding any VAT to other EC Member States	8		
Total value of all acquisitions of goods and related services excluding any VAT from other EC Member States	9		
DECLARATION: You, or someone on your behalf, must sign below			
I BRIAN ISAACS Declare that the (Full name of signatory in BLOCK LETTERS) information given above is true and complete.			
Signature .... Date 25.-11-XX A false declaration can result in prosecution			

Figure 5. Sample VAT return form

How does it work?

With just a few zero rated exceptions (listed below), goods and services carry VAT, currently charged at 17.5% or 5%. The element of VAT on the receipt given for goods purchased by you can be reclaimed. Those totals taken from your weekly accounts book go down on your VAT return form as input tax (see Figure 5).

Your total 'VATable' turnover is all turnover excluding exempt supplies. This is shown on your declaration form as net outputs. The related VAT is your output tax (examples of zero rated goods and services are shown below).

Subtract your input tax from your output tax and that is the amount owing to H M Customs and Excise.

Examples of goods and services rated at 17.5%

♦ New and used goods including hire purchase sales.

♦ Renting and hiring goods.

♦ Business stock used for private reasons.

♦ Providing a service, for example, hairdressing, decorating, etc.

♦ Charging an admission price to enter a building.

♦ Making supplies through agents.

♦ Self-employed people providing supplies, for example, some salespeople and subcontractors.

Examples of goods and services rated at 5%
- Supplies of fuel and power used in the home and by charities.

- Electricity and gas (including cylinder gas such as calor).

- Coal and solid fuels.

- Heating oils and supplies of heat and air conditioning.

Examples of zero rated goods and services
- Most food (excluding food and drink purchased in restaurants, cafes and hot take away food and drink).

- Books and newspapers.

- Young children's clothing and shoes.

- Goods being exported out of the country.

- Sales and long leases of new homes.

> **VAT is a tax you add to goods and services payable by the end purchaser.**

Examples of 'exempt supplies'
- Selling, leasing and letting land and buildings (but not lettings of garages, parking spaces or hotel and holiday accommodation).

- Insurance.

- Betting, gambling and lotteries (excluding slot machine takings).

- Providing credit.

- Certain education and training.

- The services of doctors and dentists (some are excluded, e.g. osteopaths).

- Certain undertaker services.

VAT is collected by you and sent on the due date to HM Customs and Excise. It is, therefore, their money and in order to ensure that it does not get mixed up with other monies, do as I do and open another bank or building society account, preferably one that pays a small amount of interest and at the same time allows you immediate access to your money – you will find that it is the best tonic for a good night's sleep.

BANKING

The major high street banks all offer services to the new business: advice, seminars, special deals, insurance, pensions and, as we discussed earlier, borrowing facilities. All new businesses must have a current account, so before you deposit your hard earned cash it is worth spending some time investigating the latest premium offer. A good one to start with is two years' free banking, but check the small print, you don't want to be paying extra in year three to make up for it.

Having opened your account and received your first business cheque book and paying in book, it is time to stand back and savour the moment, because you have reached a symbolic milestone on your road to being master of your own destiny. Sorry to have to interrupt this euphoric moment with a word of warning: your money is as secure as is possible once inside the bank's vault, but getting it there can necessitate some security planning:

♦ Never discuss your banking times with your staff, friends or indeed with anyone.

♦ Change your route to the bank regularly.

♦ Avoid taking money to the bank alone.

♦ Use the bank's night safe facility if your business hours force you to bank after hours.

♦ Never leave money, cheque book or credit cards in your vehicle, not even while you are paying to park.

♦ Always carry money as inconspicuously as possible.

♦ Lock yourself in your car when travelling to the bank and make a visual check when parked before you unlock.

♦ Park as close to the bank as possible and no detours.

♦ Check the opening hours – do not stand outside the bank waiting for it to open, you will become a criminal's prime target.

Bank statements

A bank statement is a record of your bank transactions, that is amounts you have paid out and amounts you have paid in, for a given period. Items will appear regularly on your bank statement that are missing from your accounts book, such as bank interest payments or direct debit payments. It is important to enter these in your books so as to avoid a lengthy search when you are unable to reconcile your accounts. A good idea is to ask for a weekly statement instead of the normal monthly one, as this will not only make you aware of your current financial state but will also help to keep you on top of your workload. On receipt of your bank statement, tick each item as it is entered in your books with a coloured pen, that way it can easily be identified and dealt with.

STATUTORY AND ADVISABLE FILE RETENTION

It is a perfectly normal human reaction to be tidy and to dispose of objects that clutter our organised lives. The business person has to think very carefully before destroying anything that relates to the business.

It is the legal duty of a business to retain the following files and documents, for a minimum of seven years:

1. VAT records including VAT returns.
2. Bank statements.
3. Sales invoices.
4. Receipts for purchases and payments.
5. Accounts and related documents.

Advisable files to retain are:

1. Staff time sheets.
2. Business department comparison figures.
3. Weekly/monthly and annual comparison figures.
4. Sales performance analysis statistics.
5. Wage analysis statistics.

SELECTING AN ACCOUNTANT

Assuming you have no prior ideas or preferences regarding the selection of your accountant, this section may help you in your search. Just because a person sets out their business stall and places the word 'accountant' over the door, it does not necessarily signify a formal accountancy qualification. Start-up businesses or small businesses should look for an accountant with one of the following organisations' letters after the name:

1. The Association of Chartered Certified Accountants – the letters ACCA or FCCA after their name.

2. The Association of Authorised Public Accountants – the letters AAPA or FAPA after their name.

3. The Institute of Chartered Accountants in England and Wales and The Institute of Chartered Accountants in Ireland – the letters FCA or ACA after their name.

4. The Institute of Chartered Accountants of Scotland – the letters CA after their name.

Recommendation is by far the best way to select an accountant. Friends, the bank manager or the Enterprise Agency will help, and don't be afraid to **negotiate the price**.

As stated earlier, lack of financial control and bad bookkeeping are major contributors to a new business's failure. I hope that this chapter has focused your mind on matters often pushed aside in the adrenaline rush that a good business idea can precipitate. So often budding entrepreneurs have entered my office at the Enterprise Agency with business ideas that can only be described as stunning, innovative and, in some cases, brilliant. I will advise them and, if necessary, place them on a business training programme. If, as is often the case, they are unable to spare the time, I will arrange for them to attend a business start-up seminar funded by one of the major high street banks.

Can you imagine how much it pleases me as a business advisor, to sce the business take off, to read about it in the local press and to smile with pleasure as my client drives past me in his new car? And can you imagine the sadness I feel when I read that the business has failed after just a short time?

**Bright ideas in isolation are not good enough.
You must have all aspects of the business under control.**

8

Computers and the Internet

DO YOU NEED A COMPUTER?

Certain businesses, for example a window cleaning business with a minimum of bookkeeping, may consider a computer an expensive toy. Apart from the cost involved, computers can be time wasting and frustrating. Many a PC has started life in the office and ended life in the cupboard. As more and more homes go online, the advantages to some businesses are obvious, but can the cost be justified for the small start-up business? Let us investigate.

What are the benefits of a computer to a small business?

◆ Improved stock control.

◆ Communication via the Internet (explained in detail later in this chapter).

◆ Speedier invoicing = improved cash flow.

◆ A convenient bookkeeping system.

◆ Word processing capability (beats a typewriter).

◆ Provided the data in a spreadsheet is entered accurately, any mathematics will be correct.

If your business requires a large amount of invoicing per month, a computerised bookkeeping system can save a great deal of time and work. If you have one or more staff, a wages package can furnish you with payslips, cheques and all the relevant information your employees need to receive.

COMPUTER TRAINING

There are a number of computer training systems; local colleges give excellent courses, as do specialist computer training centres. Contact your local Enterprise Agency or Business Link to find the nearest one to you. Self education is becoming more and more popular, and books, magazines and videos are great for those people with the self discipline to use them. Regardless of the education system you use, you are likely to find the following areas useful:

1. Word processing
2. Spreadsheets
3. Desktop publishing
4. Databases
5. Accounts
6. Computer aided design
7. Computer security
8. Communications.

BUYING A COMPUTER

For the first-time buyer, choosing the right computer can be a harrowing experience and requires a little patience, a lot of help and a fair amount of money. Magazines such as *Which Computer?* will point you in the right direction. Here are some valuable tips for a start-up business considering the purchase of a computer for office use:

◆ Although you can get by without the latest computer, reject any PC built before 1995, as accessing the Internet would be painfully slow, if possible at all. You require a minimum of 166 megahertz to be on the safe side.

◆ 64Mb RAM (that is the internal memory capacity of your computer) is a minimum requirement.

◆ The larger the screen the better, and smaller than 17" should be avoided if possible.

◆ Telephone backup is essential. It is often the case that computer operator errors can easily be rectified for the cost of a phone call, but beware – check the rate that the helpline is charging you; £1 a minute is not uncommon but is unacceptable. Test the system before you purchase; phone the helpline and if you are made to wait any more than 15 minutes start looking elsewhere.

Clearly, purchasing from a high street shop is the simplest method and will give you greater peace of mind. The advantages are:

◆ You are able to try out or have demonstrated a large number of different computers.

◆ Credit terms are usually available.

◆ Serious after sale problems can be better addressed face to face.

Disadvantages are:

◆   You will pay more.

◆   Generally speaking, you will be sold a complete package that cannot necessarily be tailored to your requirements. The package will probably include a set of software, plus hardware peripherals such as a printer and scanner.

◆   Most salespeople are not technicians and may not be able to answer all your questions.

Magazines, independent computer specialists, mail order companies, online retailers and even open markets are now retailing computer packages. The advantage of shopping around and purchasing from such a retailer is that you will probably save money. The disadvantage is that, in the main, they lack the same degree of after sales service infrastructure.

If you want to try before you buy, ask a friend. They will probably be delighted to show off their computer and Internet skills. Alternatively, for a small charge, you can hire the equipment in a cybercafe, along with an experienced instructor. Try sending an e-mail or logging on to a web browser, you will soon be hooked.

For connection to the Internet you will require the following:

◆   a computer
◆   a modem

◆　a phone line
◆　an ISP (Internet service provider).

Modems

A modem is used to transmit data between two computers over a telephone line. Purchase the fastest modem you can afford to buy; 56 kbps will fit the bill nicely. Basically, there are two distinct types of modem:

1. **Internal**. This type of modem is fitted inside the computer. Almost any new PC will come with an internal modem.

2. **External**. This type of modem sits by the side of your computer and is simply plugged in. Their only real advantage is that often a fault can be rectified by simply turning the modem off and on, impossible for the average user with an internal modem.

Getting connected

You will need a phone line. It is not essential to have a separate phone line to connect you to the Internet, but you will not be able to receive voice calls while you are online, so if you will be online for long periods, you will probably need a second line. If you decide to have another line installed, check with British Telecom and with the cable companies to ensure you get the package that best suits your pocket and your requirements.

What will a computer cost in time and money?

Around £1,000 for a state-of-the-art, medium priced system.

◆ To fully understand the computer you will need to take a course. These courses range from the free local college course to the full blown computer training centre with courses priced at between £300 and £500.

An excellent alternative is the Open University course which provides impartial advice and demonstrations in one-day seminars, aimed at the beginner.

Grants are available for small businesses towards assessing how useful a computer system might be to their business.

Accountancy software
Take your accountant's advice on which software package best satisfies your requirements. Listed below are some of the many software accounting package manufacturers and their contact numbers:

Sage Accounting	Tel: 0191 294 3000
Anagram System	Tel: 01403 259551
Money Manager	Tel: 0845 644 4555
Global 3000	Tel: 01628 551400
Quick Books Intuit	Tel: 0208 990 5500
Computer Associates	Tel: 01753 577733

SOME DO'S AND DON'TS

◆ Check the information the computer salesperson gives you. They are likely to sell you the package that earns them the most commission, which may not be the best package for you. Take independent advice.

◆ Never trust the computer memory, it will crash sooner or later. Always keep a backup of your files on a floppy disk or CD or elsewhere.

◆ Keep your back up files in a dry and secure place.

◆ Ensure you have an extension lead with a power surge trip.

◆ Lock any confidential files with password access only.

◆ To conserve memory space, delete unwanted files regularly.

◆ Defragment and clean the drives regularly (your PC can be scheduled to run these tasks for you).

THE INTERNET

Any attempt to explain the Internet in detail is not only beyond the *ability* or the remit of this author but, thankfully, it is unnecessary for the majority of people starting up in business. Without doubt the Internet is the most comprehensive and user-friendly electronic data highway ever invented, with more than *100* million users, and growing. Since the birth of mankind communication has been the key to success, not just in the field of commerce but in battle, politics and just about every endeavour primitive and modern man alike have turned their hand to.

A major revolution has taken place in our lifetime; the world of information and communication technology will never be the same. So many times I have heard people say

'I don't understand the Internet – who needs it?' Until it is pointed out to them just how much time and money they will save, they continue to bury their heads in the sand. It is essential to understand the many and diverse ways in which the Internet can speed up and improve your business.

Let me try a simple test.

		yes	no
1.	Do you have relatives or business overseas?	☐	☐
2.	Will your business require you to import or export?	☐	☐
3.	Do you use a fax machine?	☐	☐
4.	Does your business use the postal service?	☐	☐
5.	Does your business require you to travel?	☐	☐
6.	Does your business advertise?	☐	☐
7.	Are you always on the lookout for cheaper or better suppliers?	☐	☐
8.	Do you monitor your market and your competition?	☐	☐

If you can answer 'yes' to any of the above questions then the Internet has major advantages for you and your business.

GETTING ONLINE

Once you have your computer, modem and connection, you need to sign up with an ISP.

Selecting an Internet service provider (ISP)

An Internet service provider is an organisation that offers Internet services that include connection to the Internet as well as website hosting. To sign up with an ISP is relatively simple – send for or pick up from practically any high street store a free CD-ROM, load it into your PC and the on-screen instructions will guide you through. The entire operation will take you about five minutes. That is the easy part, the hard part is deciding which ISP to sign up with (there are over 200 to choose from). Just as with the mobile phone network providers, there are many different tariffs that need to be investigated to ensure you are getting the best possible deal. Many ISPs appear to be free of charge; try phoning their help line, it might cost you 50p per minute and you will be amazed at just how long it can take to address your problem. Speak to friends and other business people, before you finally decide.

E-MAIL (ELECTRONIC MAIL)

Electronic mail or e-mail is a mechanism for sending messages across a computer network. Allow me to demonstrate, from my own experience, just one of the many ways e-mail first impressed me. My only sister lives in Colorado, United States. Consequently, apart from the odd extremely expensive phone call or the even rarer letter, communication was limited. But now I can take a photograph of my family and my sister will receive it in less than five minutes at a cost of about 2p. Messages take less than one minute to send at a cost of about 1p. And the benefits are not limited to your personal life. For the small business the savings over a year are considerable. The trick is to read and write your e-mail off-line, then log on to send it; that way you are online for the shortest possible time.

Strengths

◆ Ease of use: far less troublesome than a fax, less expensive and a lot less work than a letter.

◆ Unlike with a phone call, the recipient does not have to be immediately obtainable.

◆ It does not require preliminary small talk.

◆ With the aid of an Internet webcam, costing around £30.00, you are able to see as well as speak to the recipient.

◆ Eliminates disappearing office mail or faxes.

◆ Photos, documents, even animated greetings cards, can be sent by e-mail.

◆ The use of e-fax (faxing to and from your computer) does away with another piece of office equipment, the fax machine.

◆ A fax machine automatically prints, e-fax allows the recipient to make that decision.

Weaknesses

◆ Junk mail (spam) is becoming a problem.

◆ Computer viruses are carried this way (anti-virus scanning software can be purchased to protect your computer, although the modern computer has a pre-loaded virus protection program).

◆ Incompatible systems can cause problems.

◆ It is less personal than a telephone call.

◆ The recipient has to be online to collect e-mail.

SEARCH ENGINES

A search engine is a software tool that enables the user to locate a web page that relates to one or more keywords the user has typed in. To locate a website, simply type a key word or short phrase into the box on your screen, trying to avoid the use of words such as 'and', 'the', etc. Listed below are some popular search engines:

◆ Lycos   www.lycos.co.uk
◆ Alta Vista   www.altavista.com
◆ Hotbot   www.hotbot.com
◆ Webcrawler   www.webcrawler.com
◆ All the web   www.alltheweb.com
◆ Google   www.google.com
◆ Yahoo!   www.yahoo.co.uk
◆ Ask Jeeves   www.askjeeves.com
◆ Monstercrawler   www.monstercrawler.com

ONLINE BANKING

As little as ten years ago, the idea of sitting at home and, at the touch of a button or two, having the facility to transfer money, pay bills, get account balances, etc, would have been considered science fiction. The idea of being able to talk to anyone, anywhere in the world via a small hand-held gadget made good viewing in the hit TV series *The Man from Uncle*, but once again was considered to be cloud cuckoo land.

Today, thanks to mobile phones, we can communicate with almost anyone, nearly anywhere and thanks to the

Internet we can access our bank account information from the comfort of our home.

Setting up for online banking

Although the signing up procedure varies slightly depending which bank or building society you do business with, the basic principle remains the same. Log on to your bank's website – the address should be on all the bank's literature. If that is unavailable type the name of your bank into a search engine. In a short space of time the home or first page of your bank's website will appear. Look for a link to 'online banking' or something similar and follow the instructions on screen. You will need a password to be typed in every time you wish to access account information. **It's as simple as that.**

You might also wish to consider online banks that only do business on the Internet. They claim to pass on the savings they make from not having branches to the customer.

SETTING UP A WEBSITE

The Internet can be a cost-effective method of improving your business. Apart from the mass of information at your fingertips, can it help you sell your product or service?

Depending on the type and scale of your proposed business, Internet advertising and selling requires you to have your own website. This can range from the fairly low-key one page to the all singing, all dancing multi-page production, and prices range from nil to £3000.00. Web pages can be built at home, but in my experience, they are amateurish, boring and non-effective. If you think your business can benefit from a website, then go to a professional, someone who will design a site worthy of your product or service. Pay a visit to your local Enterprise Agency, they will be able to help you contact a web designer in your area. You need to consider whether your website will service just to advertise your services, or whether you want customers to be able to order online. For a great deal more information on how to make the Internet work for you, purchase or borrow from your local library a copy of *The Daily Telegraph Electronic Business Manual.*

POINTS TO NOTE

◆ Obey the Data Protection Act. Privacy has become a very big issue.

◆ Beware of other businesses offering help – there is no such thing as a free lunch.

◆ Junk mail (spam) can be a problem.

◆ Organised crime is now focusing on the Internet as a source of easy money. Beware of revealing credit card details to sites that are not secure.

Love it or hate it, the computer is yet another tool designed to make our lives easier, more enjoyable and better informed. If you are reluctant to learn about computer technology and how it can help your business, think about our great great grandparents, who looked at the motor car and said, 'You'll never get me in one of those contraptions!'

9

Choosing Your Business Premises

In Chapter 3, a number of businesses suitable to be operated from home were suggested. Clearly that option would be impossible for most manufacturing or storage based businesses and inadvisable for any business that is image sensitive.

WORKING FROM HOME

It is fair to say that if your type of business is suitable, if your family agree and if you have the self discipline and motivation to operate your business from home, then there can be no better or more cost-effective way to commence self-employment. Don't think of it as a soft option though, you will have to put just as much time and effort into making your business a success as would be required if you were working from any other location. Many businesses run from home without planning permission. Generally speaking, they are inconspicuous micro-businesses that do nothing to inconvenience the neighbours or alert the authorities. However, to remain legal and above board or if you need to make any alterations to your home, planning permission should be sought. If you are not sure, simply contact your local Planning Officer for help, advice and information on the current application fee. If your business is as low key as that of a jewellery designer for example, you may well be considered exempt.

The Inland Revenue will generally accept a claim for anything to do with the business, for example, a proportion of the telephone bill, a proportion of heating and lighting and even security if it applies. Your accountant will be able to advise you what you can claim as costs to your business.

Advantages
- Cost.
- Convenience.
- Flexibility.

Disadvantages
- Can disrupt family life.

- Separation of business and personal life becomes more difficult.

- You may give your business a less professional image.

- A less businesslike atmosphere.

- Can create an insurance problem.

- Can create a mortgage problem (check with your mortgage provider).

- Depending on the type of business, it can create a health and safety problem (contact the Health and Safety department at your town hall or civic centre).

- ◆ Can create a planning problem (contact your planning department).

- ◆ You may be liable for capital gains tax on the sale of your home if you claim for part of your mortgage (check with your accountant).

Whilst it may appear that the disadvantages outweigh the advantages, remember that the advantages, albeit only three, are definite and large, whereas the disadvantages present only possible problems. If it is possible to run your proposed business from home, bearing in mind the above disadvantages, then I would advise you to do it.

MANAGED WORKSPACE AND SMALL BUSINESS CENTRES

Shared facilities and infrastructure make managed workspace and small business centres an attractive proposition for the small business. Access to expensive equipment such as a computer, fax machine or photocopier can soften the blow of your business start-up costs. In many instances a shared secretary can take messages for you when you are not available. This option is worth investigating.

RENTED PREMISES

Searching for the right premises should start the moment your business idea forms in your mind. It can be a long and difficult process to find working space that is in the right location and is the right size for your chosen business. In addition, the legal process can throw up all sorts of problems that require solving before final agreement can be reached with the landlord or the landlord's agent. It doesn't hurt to put the feelers out to commercial property agents informing them of your business requirements and the price ceiling you are prepared to pay. Listed below are the places you can start your property search:

◆ commercial property agents
◆ Local Enterprise Agencies
◆ the local library
◆ local authorities.

Before viewing any properties ensure that the following points are clear in your mind.

1. Cost
◆ Premium requested.
◆ Lease length.
◆ Amount of Business Rate applicable.
◆ Service charge if any.
◆ Possible fitting out costs.
◆ Installation costs: computer, phone, fire protection equipment, security etc.
◆ Advance rent.
◆ Surveyor's fees.
◆ Legal fees.

2. Minimum space required
Ask for an internal area diagram and superimpose outlines of your equipment onto it to ensure you have adequate space for the use you are planning. (Contact your local Health and Safety officer to establish the office space requirement per employee.)

3. Access benefits

Position, as I have already pointed out, is of the utmost importance. Consider whether you need the following:

- Parking facility.
- Delivery facility.
- Bus stop and railway station nearby.

4. Fixtures and fittings

Check for the following; the more you find the bigger the potential saving:

- Adequate telephone points (check their position).
- Adequate electricity points (check their position).
- Adequate lighting.
- Heating and ventilation.
- Security.
- Computer wiring.
- Room partitions.
- Fire-fighting equipment and current certificate.

BUYING A LEASE

Leasing a premises is the favoured option of most start-up businesses, the reason being that a premises can be leased for a relatively low cost and a short-term commitment. Local authorities are a good place to look, as they quite often have their own properties to let and in most cases are considered to be good landlords. Shop and supermarket notice boards occasionally display advertisements for private property deals. Business Link, your local Chamber of Commerce and your local Enterprise Agency are all also worthy of investigation in the hunt to find the right base from which to operate.

And finally a search through the local newspapers, *Daltons Weekly* advertiser and the *Yellow Pages* will give you of a list of the commercial property agents in and around your area. To search further afield, the Internet is by far the most efficient method. If at all possible try for a new lease, as the premium payable is generally a great deal lower and a rent-free period is negotiable if internal fixtures and fittings are required. Once the lease terms are agreed and signed it is very difficult to make changes, so any negotiating should take place at an early stage. Employing a solicitor is a wise move and if the lease makes you, the tenant, responsible for maintenance and repairs to the property, employ a chartered surveyor to ensure that any work required is paid for by the landlord prior to your agreeing and signing any legally binding document. Your local Business Enterprise Agency will give you advice, as well as a list of chartered surveyors and solicitors. A free leaflet, available from the Department of the Environment, entitled 'Business Leases and Security of Tenure' can assist you in your negotiations.

A change of use of the premises will, under certain circumstances, require planning permission. For example, to change a shop to a cafe or restaurant can be a lengthy and expensive process. If you are considering a catering business, under no circumstances should you commit yourself to any lease agreement until you have acquired a change of use consent from the planning authority.

Security of tenure
When you reach the end of your lease, you can remain in your premises at the same rent until the appropriate steps

under the Landlord and Tenant Act of 1954 have been taken. The landlord cannot just ask you to leave. You must have six months' notice in writing. There are two main grounds for repossession by the landlord:

1. Because you are an unsatisfactory tenant (this can be challenged in a court of law).

2. Because the landlord has other plans for the property.

Rent reviews

These are normally scheduled between three and five years, regardless of the length of the lease. Take care to check how they are calculated. If you are not sure, employ a solicitor.

Legal checklist

1. Is the lease the property of the vendor?

2. Can the premises be used for the business you are proposing to run?

3. Are there any planning restrictions on the premises? (conservation area, listed building, etc)?

4. What is the length of the lease?

5. Can you sublet all or part of the premises?

6. On what date are the rent reviews, if any?

7. What insurance responsibilities are you being asked to agree?

8. What, if any, are your lease renewal rights?

9. What are the landlord's costs and who will be asked to pay them?

Numbers four to nine inclusive are all **negotiable**.

Selling the lease

Take great care to read and understand your rights. Should you wish to surrender or assign the lease, a landlord cannot unreasonably withhold permission. However, landlords can impose severe financial preconditions, such as making you responsible for any future unpaid rent. The landlord will, of course, want references from any prospective assignee.

FINALLY

There is a very old saying in the retail business:

> 'There are only three important things for retailing, they are position, position and position'.

You are better paying a little more rent to be where your customers are, than paying low rent tucked away out of sight. Whilst that may well apply to retail, other businesses require only storage, office or warehouse space. But whatever premises your business needs to trade in, take every precaution, seek professional advice and check the negotiation progression at every stage.

10

Sales Techniques and Marketing

SALES TECHNIQUES

It was Henry Ford who first stated 'nothing happens until a sale is made'. How true, and how often it is that the sale is left in the hands of an untrained person. Mr Ford may well have had the manufacturing capability to produce cars at a phenomenal rate, but if they did not get sold, production capability was of no value at all. Contrary to popular belief, sales methods and techniques can be learnt just like any other subject.

Large companies spend fortunes on advertising their products, fortunes on lavish shops to attract the customer and fortunes on window and in-store displays, only to lose valuable sales through a lack of ongoing product sales training.

This chapter aims to improve your selling skills and, should your business grow and you employ staff to sell, provides you with some ideas to pass on to them.

Broadly speaking, a salesperson must have the following skills and attributes:

1. Job satisfaction.

2. Product knowledge.

3. Enthusiasm.

4. Formal and up-to-date sales technique training.

5. The ability to ascertain the customer's needs.

6. The ability to fit the product to the customer.

7. The ability to recognise the customer's problems, e.g. shortage of money, shortage of time, or just plain boredom.

8. The ability to recognise the time to close the sale.

9. A likeable and friendly manner.

10. Last, but by no means least, a clean and smart appearance.

Before we go any further let me hit you with a few 'don'ts':

1. Don't be aggressive, avoid the hard sell.

2. Don't talk about yourself, it holds no interest for the customer.

3. Don't approach the customer smelling of alcohol, cigarettes or anything that the customer may find the slightest bit offensive.

4. Don't ever argue with the customer, simply ask questions.

5. If you get a positive buying signal from the customer, cease your sales presentation – to continue can lose you the sale.

6. Don't criticise others.

7. Don't criticise other manufacturers' products.

During the mid 1950s a revolution occurred in the technique of selling. From across the Atlantic came new ideas and ways to successfully sell the ever increasing range of consumer goods being made available in the UK. AIDA had arrived – I will explain shortly.

Have you ever walked into a store to make a major purchase, such as a TV, a bed, washing machine or refrigerator, and been pounced upon by an enthusiastic, commission-orientated salesperson who uses those magic words 'Can I help you?' I wonder just how many times you have answered 'I'm just looking, thank you'. End of sale. All the hopes and aspirations of the manufacturer and their design, distribution, advertising, sales promotion and display have ended in failure because the untrained salesperson asked the wrong question. The inexperienced salesperson asked a positive question, to which they received a positive answer. (It's fair to say that the above is far less likely to happen in the smaller and more training-orientated privately owned business than the large multi-outlet retailer.)

The salesperson should have approached the customer, giving a reasonable length of time for the customer to settle on the product group of interest, and then opened the conversation with a statement. If, for example, the customer had shown interest in the range of vacuum cleaners, the salesperson's approach may well have been, 'That cleaner has a five year parts and labour guarantee'.

This is a statement of fact that completes the customer approach without rejection and allows the salesperson to continue to speak to the customer.

AIDA is a logical sequence through which the salesperson and the customer must travel to reach a successful sale.

A is for attention

Give the customer your attention. Allow enough time for the customer to show interest in a particular product group, but remember that allowing too much time can lead to the customer leaving the shop through lack of salesperson attention. Verbally highlight a sales feature.

I is for interest

Show interest in the customer's needs. Verbally list the sales features and at the same time begin to establish the customer's needs by questioning. For example:

♦ What type of vacuum cleaner do you use, is it an upright type or a cylinder type?

♦ Do you have a large or small house?

♦ Do you have any pets in your house?

This type of questioning helps the salesperson to ensure the customer will go home with the right product to suit their requirements, thus cutting down the risk of losing the sale or having the product returned at a later date.

D is for desire

The desire for the customer to own the product builds as the salesperson marries the product sales features to the needs of the customer. For example:

♦ You mentioned you had two dogs – the selection of tools provided with the machine will make light work of the hair they leave on your carpet.

♦ As your home is on three levels the comparatively low weight of this product makes it a good choice for you.

♦ The rechargeable option is certainly a big plus when you travel on holiday in your caravan.

A is for action

It's crunch time, the point at which you have to ask the customer to purchase the product, the point of no return and the pinnacle of all the work, time, effort and money that is now at risk. A simple mistake can ruin the sale, so what do you do? How do you bring the sale to a successful conclusion? There are three main methods used to close a sale:

1. Dual positive suggestion

Children are blessed with the ability to close a sale without their even knowing it, simply by asking a dual positive question, that is to say asking two questions that both have a positive answer. For example, little Robert says, 'Mum shall we go to the movies today or will tomorrow suit you better?' Either answer gets Robert to the movies.

Here are a few examples of dual positive suggestions that can help you close the sale:

◆ Would you like us to deliver, or did you want to take it with you?

◆ Will you be paying cash, or can I show you our credit terms?

◆ Do you prefer the pink or the white one?

◆ Would you like to purchase it with tools or without at a reduced price?

2. The concession method
Suggesting a larger quantity, knowing the customer will settle for a little less, will often close the sale.

3. The silent method
Having reached the end of the sales presentation, the skilful salesperson will go silent and remain that way, and the customer will feel obliged to speak and will order. (Only the experienced salesperson should attempt to use this method, as it can backfire.)

Overcoming objections
During any sales presentation, there is always the likelihood that an objection by the customer will raise its ugly head. That objection can be turned into a positive sales aid by the skilful salesperson. Recognising the true objection will point you in the right direction. Take, for example, a mother attempting to purchase a dress for her young daughter. 'This dress doesn't fit,' says the young girl, believing her mum is more likely to accept that than

the real reason, which is the little girl doesn't like the colour. Our experienced salesperson knows the dress is a perfect fit and immediately recognises the ploy. To attempt to convince the little girl would be time consuming and may well end up with a lost sale. The salesperson offers the young girl the same dress in another colour, hopefully one she likes. The moral of the story is don't fight the objection, learn to 'go with the flow'.

A full-scale training session in sales techniques might require the class to break down into pairs and practise selling to one another under the watchful eye of a video camera. Playing the tape back highlights the errors and helps you correct any mistakes. A natural approach to the customer is vital and will come with practice. Many sales courses are available, simply contact your local Enterprise Agency for further details.

SELLING WHOLESALE

A book of products, some samples and an order book are the basic requirements for the sales representative, or in the case of a one-person business, you!

Guidelines

1. Do make an appointment.

2. Do ensure your products are packaged as the end user will see them.

3. Have any discounts available clearly in your mind, state your price, and outline your terms of trading.

4. Be sure you are aware of your competitors' prices and terms.

TELEPHONE SALES

However annoying we find it when we are called on the phone by a salesperson, it is a very successful sales method and deserves serious consideration. If you believe your business can benefit from telesales, BT publish two guides, *Talking Better Business* and *Talking Better Business Essentials*. The Mailing Preference Service makes available lists of people who do not wish to be contacted by telephone.

SMALL-SCALE SELLING

Boot sales, craft fairs and market stalls all offer an opportunity to test market your products cheaply and are generally well patronised. They have put many budding entrepreneurs on the road to fame and fortune. For further information contact your local town hall or civic centre or check out the advertisements in the local press.

MARKETING

A question I am often asked is: 'What, if any, is the difference between marketing and selling?' Marketing is the umbrella name that describes the process that starts with research, moves on to product planning and development and ends with sales promotion. Selling is the negotiation and final exchange of goods or services for payment. Marketing and sales must always work together but are not interchangeable. Marketing's main target is to make people aware of your goods and services, so try to tailor your marketing strategy in order to obtain maximum effectiveness.

Market research

This is the process by which you are able to establish, through data collection, collation and analysis, information which will assist you in making business decisions on all aspects of marketing and selling your product or service. It is not essential to employ a professional market research company, it is easy to do yourself and considerably cheaper. Standing in the high street with a clipboard is one method of carrying out research, but more information can be gained by looking through the relevant books in your local library. Test marketing a product can be achieved simply by renting a table at a boot sale.

Market research will assist in answering the following questions:

1. Who buys your and your competitors' products? When and why do they buy them?

2. Has the market increased or decreased in recent years?

3. How can you improve your product or service?

4. Is it low price that sells your product? (If it is, beware of the price cutters.)

5. Is it packaging and sales promotion that sells your product?

6. Do your competitors have a larger market share than you? If so, why?

7. What marketing methods do your competitors use?

8. What alterations can you make to your product or service to increase your sales?

9. Will product diversification increase your share of the market?

Window display

If you are a retailer, your potential customer's first impression of your shop is of the utmost importance. An eye-catching display will encourage the customer to give your shop window more than a cursory glance, which hopefully will lead them to open your shop door and enter.

Think of a successful shop in your main shopping area; does it have dirty windows, low lights, dusty stock on display, a cat asleep in the corner and metal security grills left down all day? I think not; it is far more likely to have fresh clean goods that are well displayed and brightly lit.

Pricing must be clear, precise and uniform. Check with your local Trading Standards Office for any statutory obligation when displaying hire purchase terms. There are shopkeepers who believe that showing no prices in the window encourages people to enter and ask the price, but from my experience suspicion drives the potential customer away.

ADVERTISING

Advertising can be selective or non-selective. With selective advertising the aim is to target a specific group identified through questionnaires, or through market research undertaken by yourself or purchased from a market research company. Non-selective advertising follows the AIDA method explained previously.

1. Attract the Attention of the reader.

2. Capture the Interest of the reader.

3. Generate a Desire for your product or service.

4. Precipitate the Action of purchase.

Advertising is a highly specialised business and, provided your funds run to it, you would be well advised to employ professionals in design and layout, production and distribution.

Places to advertise
◆   Local radio.
◆   Local TV.
◆   Local cinema.
◆   Local shops.
◆   Local newspapers and directories.
◆   Specialist papers and magazines.

If, however, funds are restricted for advertising, let's consider the alternatives:

Mailshots
Mailshots are those aggravating pieces of paper that drop through your letter box. They have a very low response rate but are a very popular form of advertising. Selective mailshots are the most effective, but that can involve you in hours of tedious work tracking down the potential customer.

Leaflets

As with mailshots, once the artwork has been completed, distribution problems take over the headache number one spot. Newspapers will deliver leaflets at a relatively low cost per unit, and private armies of youngsters can deliver locally at a cost, but the downside with this method is you very rarely know exactly how many find their way through the letterbox and how many end up in the rubbish bin. It would be effective if you were able to target areas and be sure the leaflets reached their destination. If you use my method you can do just that at a very low cost. Here's how it works.

In every city, town, or village in the country, political party workers from the three major parties each distribute between one and three leaflets per year. In the past, funding for the leaflets presented no real problem and advertising on the leaflets was unnecessary. These days, however, finances are not as easily come by and low-key advertising has become the accepted norm.

The advantages are:

1. Relatively low cost.

2. A much higher percentage of leaflets hit the target letterboxes.

3. Political leaflets tend to lie about longer in the home than ordinary advertising leaflets.

4. You are able to specify areas where your leaflets are to be distributed.

Press releases

It's not often in life that the cheapest is the best but free advertising in the form of a press release is possibly the best method of getting your message out. If you are planning a new product, a new retail outlet or even a visit by a famous or local celebrity, phone the press. Quite often they have trouble filling the pages of their newspaper and will welcome your story with open arms.

Leaflets

Much has been written about the humble leaflet; authors have attempted to tell the reader the optimum size and the best colour paper to use. One author even insisted on informing the reader of a method of folding that ensured the leaflet landed the right way up on the mat.

The reality is that the type of image you wish your business to project will very much determine the type of paper, the style of script and the colours used. For example, a one-person gardening business requires little more than black print on a white A4 sheet to outline the services on offer. The same format used by a building surveyor may well reduce his chances of persuading a potential client to pick up the phone. A computer (see Chapter 8) and some basic software, such as Coral Print House or Microsoft Desktop Publisher, allow us all to design and publish our own leaflets. A trip to the local photocopying service will produce a printed one sided leaflet for around £15 a thousand, that is 1.5p per letterbox, cheap by any standards.

Websites

Once again the success of this form of advertising largely depends on the type of business you are contemplating. The cost involved may prove to be too much for what may turn out to be an image boost or, at the worst, an expensive ego trip for you. The web is a powerful advertising tool, just make sure it is the right one. (See Chapter 8 for more information.)

Exhibitions

Hotels and exhibition halls are often the venue chosen to show your goods and services. Customers and potential customers are invited to attend to view and hopefully order. As well as providing promotional material, you and your staff are on hand to answer any questions relating to the products, pricing, delivery dates and even discounts. The results may not necessarily be immediate but should be assessed over the following six months.

Public relations

I have chosen to list public relations under marketing because I firmly believe it is a powerful advertising tool. Whether you choose to invite a well-known celebrity to open your shop or sponsor a local youth football team, the benefit to the business comes from the excellent publicity that can be gained. Invite the media. Newspapers and local radio require a constant flow of new and interesting material and the article will appear as a feature rather than an advertisement. Even better it's **free**.

FINALLY

1. The best form of advertising is still word of mouth recommendation.

2. Aim for the biggest spread of advertising possible; do not limit yourself to just one method.

3. If you've got it, **flaunt it!**

(11)

Staff Selection and Security

If it is necessary for your business to employ staff, there are a number of important issues to consider.

FINDING EMPLOYEES

For many businesses the quality of their staff is the key that will unlock their success; staff can be the most valuable resource a business has. Friendly, helpful, well-trained staff are an asset that must be retained for the smooth running and efficiency of the business. Finding the right staff, however, can be an exhausting, time-consuming business. Consider the following before you recruit:

1. What qualities are needed to fit the job?

2. Will the new employee fit in with the rest of the workforce?

3. What salary are you prepared to pay?

4. What is the job description?

5. What training will be given?

6. What, if any, are the fringe benefits of the job?

There are a number of ways to attract new staff. Advertising in your local newspaper is probably the most popular method, although many employers prefer to start with their local job centre or existing employees' recommendation. Any advert should outline the job truthfully; what is the point in going through the contact, job interview and employment process, only to lose the applicant when the job does not match up to the advert? Listed below are ideas you may wish to include in your advert if they apply:

+ Good working environment.
+ Job security.
+ Promotion prospects.
+ Good pay.
+ Future business expansion.
+ Opportunity for self motivation.

Let the hopeful applicant have as much information as possible to avoid time-consuming disappointments. Here are some ideas on what to include:

+ The job description.

+ The job title (most important to many applicants).

+ The pay (important to all the applicants).

+ The location (this can involve travel, time, expense and possibly a major domestic upheaval for the family).

+ The company's future plans.

+ Job application details (and requirements such as applicant's CV, etc.).

+ The job application closing date.

THE RECRUITMENT PROCESS

Always make sure you have a properly planned job application form; not only will it provide the information you require, it will be used in the future to enable you to keep an accurate staff record. Essentially, the application form provides the employer with enough information (following reference checks) to assess the applicant, and it also forms the basis of an agreement.

A job interview allows you to select an applicant and the applicant to select you. Hopefully, the compilation of the job advertisement will sift out the unsuitable candidates, leaving only those people who are genuinely able, willing and keen to do the work and fit your job requirements. As long as you can show that your decision on who to employ is based on the applicant's ability to do the job, you cannot be accused of discrimination.

The job offer

Your letter of offer must never precede reference and medical checks. Once agreed, the letter and your job advertisement form part of the contract of employment. Putting it another way, if after sending the applicant a letter of job offer you change your mind, you had best contact your solicitor because you may find yourself in serious trouble.

The contract

In order to prepare a contract of employment you need to state:

1. Names of the parties.

2. Salary details: how much, when it is paid and by what method.

3. Overtime: how it is calculated and whether it is part of the basic pay or an extra.

4. Hours of work.

5. Job commencement date.

6. Holiday entitlement.

7. The employee's sickness entitlement.

8. Any extra job benefits (pensions, etc.).

9. Grievance procedures.

10. Disciplinary procedures.

11. Period of notice.

You should give the employee a copy of the contract no later than 13 weeks after the commencement of the job.

The new job
Make every effort to ease your new employee into the job. A training programme will help to introduce the new arrival in a more structured and acceptable way. Training can be introduced at any time, and it does not have to be formal. Over a period of say the first month, the training should be low key and cover everyday features of the job, for example:

1. Job procedures.
2. House rules.
3. Break times.

4. Fire drill.
5. Workplace geography and where to find things.

Training for the job is a continuous process and you would be wise to make the most of it. Being the new kid on the block can be a worrying experience, but team spirit and friendly faces will work wonders. Hopefully, all will be well, but what if it all goes horribly wrong?

DISMISSAL

You may dismiss an employee who has six months' service or less without a written statement. Between six months and two years a written statement is required. After two years the full disciplinary procedure must be followed. The normal disciplinary procedure is a verbal warning (noted) preceding a written warning, followed by a final written warning. Instant dismissal can follow a serious offence such as theft. It must, of course, be proven.

An employee can be dismissed for any substantial reason including redundancy, misconduct or inability to perform the job function as agreed in the contract. Employees cannot be dismissed for belonging to a trade union or for attending a trade union meeting outside of working hours. Neither can they have any action taken against them for belonging to a union, including being singled out for redundancy on the basis of their union involvement.

Minimum periods of notice

◆   Up to one month's service there is no minimum period required.

♦ Between one month and two years' service one week's notice is required.

♦ After two years, the requirement is one week's notice for each year's service. In excess of 12 years, the minimum period of notice is 12 weeks.

The employee must give one week's notice, unless he or she wishes to leave the job within the first month.

SHOP SECURITY

It is virtually impossible to make your shop premises burglar proof, but theft can be kept to a minimum. Contact your local crime prevention officer, who will be happy to assist you to plan your anti-theft measures. To start with, check with your insurance company; it may be that they are insisting you use a certain type of lock or that you fit an alarm system or security grills. (Check with town planning if you are in a conservation area, where the appearance of shopfronts is closely controlled.) Your insurance company may, depending on your trade, ask for a safe to be fitted. Having established what security measures are necessary at an early stage you now have the advantage of being able to design and cost them in with the fitting out of your shop.

A great number of security precautions are common sense. Here are some important ones:

1. Leave a light on at night.

2. Leave the empty till open at night (a thief will destroy a cash register in an effort to open it).

3. Leave only a small float overnight or better still no float at all.

4. Use the bank's night safe to bank the shop's takings.

5. Double check that the doors are locked.

Try to keep an up-to-date record of your stock, to enable an insurance claim to be processed as speedily as possible.

THEFT BY STAFF

The suspicion that a member of your staff is stealing is not good enough, you must have proof. Clearly, this creates a problem and can cause unease and bad feeling towards you. Unless you can catch the thief red-handed, consider the following:

♦ Let your staff know about the problem, after which you may find the thefts stop.

♦ Be seen to be keeping a record of stock and money.

♦ Check all incoming stock against delivery notes.

♦ Insist that the staff lock away any bags or parcels they bring to work.

♦ Insist that staff purchases must go through the cash register in the normal way.

♦ If the thefts continue contact the police.

SHOPLIFTING

Regrettably shoplifting is a growing problem and not just for the large stores or the supermarkets but for the independent shopkeeper as well. To combat the problem, common sense and some high-tech equipment may be required. Try to ensure all easily pocketable goods are either chained to the display or directly in front of the cashier. Good lighting can play an important part in the war against shoplifting. Other methods of enhancing shop security include the following:

♦ Buy or rent a closed circuit TV security system.

♦ Mirrors can be strategically placed so that the staff can watch the shop's most vulnerable areas.

♦ Security tagged items and a sensor near the door are extremely effective.

♦ If finances allow, a security guard remains the best deterrent.

A citizen's arrest, if found to be unlawful, can result in you, the shopkeeper, paying out a considerable sum in damages.

Do
1. Be vigilant.
2. Only challenge the suspect outside the premises.
3. Call the police once the goods have been found in the suspect's possession.

Don't
1. Act on suspicion only.
2. Allow your personal feelings to surface.

3. Risk physical injury to yourself or your staff.

Security checks

From time to time make the following checks:

1. Stock.
2. Cash register print roll.
3. Cash float.
4. Door locks.
5. Window locks.
6. Alarm system.
7. Price tickets.
8. Staff time sheets.
9. Make sure your premises are secure day and night.

(12)

When It All Goes Wrong

I was in two minds whether or not to include a chapter on business failure. But it is an unfortunate fact that a great number of businesses fail within the first two years.

WHY BUSINESSES FAIL

If you were to speak to a bankrupt business person, they may blame the failing on a number of different factors, for example:

- current trends (e.g. supermarket one-stop shopping)
- current fashions (out-of-date stock)
- unfair competition (large retail parks and out-of-town shopping)
- political changes
- rising costs
- price cutting
- Internet shopping
- lack of parking facilities
- cost of parking facilities.

Whatever reason a business finds itself in financial difficulties, where do you go from here? Most budding entrepreneurs don't imagine they will become bankrupt. But time moves on in the business, perhaps a few mistakes were made, perhaps you didn't work quite as hard as you needed to, perhaps you under-estimated your competitors, or perhaps you over-estimated your own ability. You may think these problems are easy to recognise, looking from the outside in, but things are not quite so clear when you are involved in the process of keeping your business alive. If you want to avoid some of these pitfalls, ask yourself:

1. Are your employees efficient and productive?
2. Do they have target figures to aim for?
3. Do you include your employees in discussions concerning the business?
4. Is your cash flow properly managed?
5. Are you pulling your weight?

THE WARNING SIGNS
1. Your cheques bounce.
2. Suppliers refuse to supply you.
3. You exceed your overdraft limit.
4. Your liabilities are greater than your assets.
5. The boss will not heed advice.
6. There is a lack of direction.
7. There is a lack of control.

If any of the above strike a chord, don't delay – seek advice immediately.

WHAT HAPPENS NEXT
The social stigma of bankruptcy remains an important factor. Business failure is surrounded by the following issues:

Bankruptcy
A debtor becomes an undischarged bankrupt as soon as

the court is satisfied there is no other alternative, such as an offer of payment to a creditor. A bankrupt is prohibited from being a company director, or managing a company, neither may a bankrupt hold the post of MP, councillor or Justice of the Peace. Furthermore, an undischarged bankrupt cannot without revealing undischarged bankruptcy obtain credit of more than £250 or engage in any business without revealing the same. Money earned by the undischarged bankrupt is the property of the trustees, which is then used to pay the creditors.

Provided the debts are less than £20,000 the bankrupt will be discharged in two years. Above that figure the bankrupt will be discharged in three years, unless they have been bankrupt within the previous 15 years, in which case they will have to wait 15 years or longer.

Receivership
Receivership applies to limited companies. Once a receiver is appointed their wide-ranging powers can override the directors and they can either run the business or sell off the assets to pay the costs (auctioneer's fees) the receiver's fees, the receiver's appointees' fees and then any other creditors.

Administration
This also applies to limited companies. Provided the company has enough funds to finance a rescue plan, administration may allow it to trade back to solvency.

Liquidation and winding up

Following the appointment of a liquidator, called the 'official receiver', the company's assets are called in and the creditors are paid in the order displayed later in this chapter.

Sheltering personal assets

This can be a risky business. If it is shown in court that the assets were hidden with the intention of placing them beyond the reach of creditors, you may well lose them.

Wrongful trading

In a worst-case scenario, the limited liability cover can be removed by the courts, leaving the directors personally liable for any debt.

At the point at which your liabilities exceed your assets you are technically insolvent, so take a close look at the warning signs on the previous pages.

If your financial position as a sole trader is such that you are unable to pay your debts now or in the future, any one of your creditors owed at least £750 unsecured is in a position to serve you with a formal demand to:

- ◆ pay the outstanding debt
- ◆ secure the outstanding debt
- ◆ arrange with the creditor an acceptable level of payment, under an agreed scheme.

The latter has proved successful in avoiding bankruptcy,

but you will need to employ an authorised insolvency practitioner to draft a legal agreement. Fees for this service must be paid in advance.

Partnership

Each partner is responsible for all of the liabilities of the business and this can cause many problems if one partner has more assets than the other.

Limited company

Under the Insolvency Act, winding up can be voluntary or administered. A voluntary resolution must have 75% of the board members' votes, and must be published in the *London Gazette*. Following a statutory declaration by the directors, which states that after investigation the company will be able to pay its debts within a 12-month period, the winding up remains a voluntary winding up and the board members can appoint the liquidator. The creditors will appoint a liquidator if the company is shown to be insolvent.

The secretary or a director of the company must provide the official receiver (usually the liquidator who is an officer of the Department of Trade and Industry) with a complete list of the assets and liabilities of the company in a sworn statement. Following a creditors' meeting a decision will be made whether to appoint a liquidator or allow the official receiver to carry out the duty. The liquidator pays the debts in the following rotation:

1. Asset secured loans and debts.
2. Winding up costs.

3. Rates, water rates, wages, salaries, and income tax.
4. Loans and debts secured on any of the company's assets and not an individual one (a floating charge).
5. Trade creditors.
6. Shareholders.

In the case of insufficient funds to pay all the creditors, a director may be made personally liable if it can be shown that the director continued to trade knowing that insolvency was inevitable.

TAKE ACTION

If in your opinion your business is unable to pay its debts in full, seek advice immediately. **Don't bury your head in the sand.** Speak to your accountant or contact a Business adviser, who will point you in the right direction for qualified help. It may well be that the advice is to take voluntary action, rather than one of your creditors starting bankruptcy proceedings against you which will involve the closing of your business.

Following bankruptcy the possibility of starting another business becomes considerably more difficult. However, for a director of a wound-up company, another attempt at business is possible unless you are deemed to be unfit.

Learn from your mistakes.

$$\begin{pmatrix} 13 \end{pmatrix}$$

Miscellaneous Information

BUSINESS INSURANCE

Only a fool would operate a business without at least the minimum of insurance cover. I have listed below just some of the disasters you frequently read about that can and do destroy uninsured businesses:

- fire
- burglary
- flood
- explosion
- subsidence
- denial of trade (can be caused by major road works, major road accidents, terrorist attack, etc.).

Although it is possible to cover individual risks, a comprehensive insurance policy is a far more sensible method of approach. For example, a shopkeeper's all-in policy would give cover for:

1. stock
2. fixtures and fittings
3. loss of profits
4. buildings
5. cash register float
6. cash in transit
7. loss of earnings (through accident or ill health)

8. public liability
9. employer's liability
10. consequential loss
11. glass window breakage (a must for shops)
12. frozen food cover
13. fidelity insurance (covers you against theft or fraud by your employees).

THE PROFESSIONALS

Insurance brokers

A good insurance broker will advise you on the type of policy that will best suit your business and seek to get you the best possible deal. Some brokers will advertise their particular speciality, and as with any major purchase it is worth shopping around.

For the home-based business, insurance should include:

1. Personal insurance (accident or illness cover is essential for the one-person business).

2. Motor vehicle insurance (check that your cover includes business use).

3. Credit insurance (bad debt cover).

4. Consequential loss (cover against loss or cessation of trade caused by loss or damage to assets).

5. Product liability (cover against faulty servicing or faulty manufacturing).

6. Asset loss or damage (check with your broker on the level of cover, if any, you have under the house policy).

Solicitors

The start-up or small business can sometimes find it prudent to seek the advice of a solicitor. Although it is not always possible, ask for a quote to enable you to budget and don't be scared to negotiate the price. If in doubt, check with your nearest Law Centre. Many solicitors belong to the Lawyers for your Business Scheme, offering a free initial consultation for start-up and young businesses, plus a quote for any further work required.

Accountants

See Chapter 7 for information on choosing an accountant.

SERVICES ON OFFER

Listed below are the services on offer by various professionals that you are most likely to use in the day-to-day running of your business as well as your start-up period:

Accountants offer:
- PAYE advice
- VAT returns
- annual accounts
- bookkeeping
- tax returns
- general business advice.

Insurance brokers offer:
- a choice of levels of insurance
- insurance advice
- some financial services.

Solicitors offer:
- partnership agreements
- Memorandum on Articles of Association
- conveyancing
- property agreements – lease or rent
- planning and change of use agreements
- litigation work.

Commercial property and estate agents offer:
- available businesses to rent, lease or purchase
- property inventories
- information on new developments.

Architects offer:
- surveys
- plans
- property advice (general).

SETTING UP AN OFFICE

Regardless of the size of your business, an office is an essential element. It may well be an open briefcase on a chair or a huge building; for the purposes of this chapter, size doesn't matter.

The essential supplies can be purchased almost anywhere and many companies deliver the goods to you free of charge.

Stationery requirements

Headed notepaper
This can often be your first contact with a potential

customer. It is wise to ensure it projects a favourable image. Try if possible to purchase paper that is 80 grams per square metre in weight and don't forget you will need plain paper of the same weight to continue a letter.

Envelopes
White for letters and brown for invoices is the norm, but there are no hard and fast rules.

Business cards
Once again, your image is on the line, so design your cards with care and always carry a good stock with you, you just never know when you are going to need them.

Compliment slips
These are small sheets of paper giving your name and address, used to accompany brochures, tickets and invoices. A small thing, but once again attention to detail reflects on your business.

Estimates
The estimate is a price the work or article will cost the customer and is quite often not the final price. Show the VAT separate, or simply quote all prices subject to VAT.

Quotations
Gives a firm price, again net of VAT.

Invoices
The invoice is, in effect, the bill and must include the following information (Figure 6):

THE ALTERNATIVE CO LTD   12 Anywhere Street
                                              Somewhere on Sea
                                                         KENT

Phone 0800 000 000
Fax 0801 020304
Email raspberry@hotmail

                                    VAT NO. 1234 5678 9

INVOICE

INVOICE NO. 001   INVOICE DATE: 01.01.02

INVOICE ADDRESS: DELIVERY ADDRESS:

Smith & Co   As per invoice
123 High Street
Anywhere

PURCHASE ORDER NO. 003 TERMS: 30 DAYS ACCOUNT REF NO: ALT65

ORDER QTY	DEL. QTY	PART NUMBER	DESCRIPTION	UNIT PRICE	TOTAL PRICE
3	3	00000kbfco	GOODS	£ 10.00	£30.00

TOTAL NET AMOUNT	£30.00
TOTAL VAT AMOUNT	£ 5.25
CARRIAGE	£0.00
INVOICE TOTAL	£35.25

Figure 6. Sample invoice.

- invoice number
- order/reference number
- the date
- the name and address of both the supplier and the purchaser
- the quantity
- the unit price
- a description of the goods or services
- the total price excluding VAT
- the VAT @ x%
- the total price including VAT
- discount (where applicable)
- postage and packing costs
- payment terms
- VAT registration number.

Statement

A statement is the balance outstanding rendered to the customer at the end of each month (see Figure 7).

Office furniture and equipment

Essential office furniture such as desks, chairs and filing cabinets can be purchased from any office equipment store and you may be able to get them second-hand.

You will probably also need:

- a photocopier (this can often be leased along with a maintenance agreement)
- a metal waste bin
- a computer (see Chapter 8 for more information)
- a printer
- a telephone.

THE ALTERNATIVE CO LTD

12 Anywhere Street
Somewhere on Sea
KENT

Phone 0800 000 000
Fax 0801 020304

STATEMENT

Smith & Co
123 High Street
Anywhere

Date: 31.01.05   Account No: ALT65   Page: 1

DATE	TYPE	REFERENCE	DEBIT	CREDIT	BALANCE
01.01.05	INVOICE	INV.001	£35.25		£35.25

TOTAL DUE £35.25

Figure 7. Sample statement.

A great number of features can now be housed in the humble telephone. Consider whether the following would be useful to you:

- automatic call back
- fast dial
- Internet access
- e-mail (send and receive)
- 200 plus name and number memory
- calculator
- caller identification
- call transfer
- fax
- answerphone
- remote playback
- loudspeaker and microphone.

It is essential to have good lighting, as bad lighting can lead to eye strain.

HEALTH AND SAFETY IN THE WORKPLACE

As the employer, it is your duty to ensure that the working environment as well as all the equipment is safe, not only for your employees but for anyone visiting your office. If you are intending to employ, here are the rules:

1. Contact your local Environmental Health Department.

2. Display the Health and Safety Law poster.

3. Ensure you have adequate employer's liability insurance.

4. Display your employer's liability insurance certificate at each place of work.

5. If you have five or more employees, show them your written policy statement on health and safety and make an assessment of the fire risks at your workplace.

The health and safety officer has power of entry to your workplace, as well as legal enforcement rights. There are no shortcuts with health and safety, the right way is the only way. Listed below are a few of the essential do's and dont's:

Do

◆ Keep fire exits clear at all times.

◆ Plan what to do in case of fire.

◆ Check all staff know the fire drill.

◆ Inspect and keep maintained all fire extinguishers and show your staff how to use them (your local fire station will issue you with instructions).

◆ Check your electrical wiring is in good condition.

◆ Use conduit to route wires and cables.

◆ Keep the first aid box in an easily accessible place and check its contents regularly.

Don't

◆ Leave wires or cables trailing from equipment.

◆ Attempt to carry heavy items – use a trolley.

◆ Stand on chairs.

◆ Place things on the floor (someone will trip over them).

- Leave filing cabinet drawers open (only open one drawer at a time).
- File anything above the head level of the shortest employee.
- Allow anyone to smoke in the workplace during working hours.

A word of advice

The old adage 'Don't spoil the ship for a hap'th of tar' applies. Without an efficient and safe office environment, mistakes may happen that could potentially cost you money. An accident to yourself or an employee may result in a great deal of time and work, as well as distress. Don't cut corners – do it properly.

PROTECTING YOUR IDEAS

Protection of intellectual property can be an expensive and highly complex process for the new business. There are only four methods of protection:

1. **Patents which protect inventions and technological innovations.**
    A patent allows an inventor to stop anyone else from copying the patented item.

2. **Copyright which protects music, art and literary works.**
    A copyright protects the unlicensed reproduction of books, paintings, films, songs, music, engineering works, plays, articles and original creative works. Infringement occurs only when a 'substantial' amount of your work is reproduced – the court will decide.

3. **Design registration which protects the appearance and shape of a product.**
   To register your design you are required to apply to the Design Registry and if your design complies with the requirements of the Registered Design Act of 1949, you will be issued with a certificate which will allow you the sole rights to manufacture, use, or sell articles of that design in business.

4. **Trade mark which protects pictures, symbols and logos.**
   The registration of a trade mark will depend on how distinctive it is; confusion with other symbols already registered would exclude it. Registration requires you to contact the Patents Office (trade mark branch) in order to check there are no areas of conflict with other trade marks. Registration is for seven years and will be processed only after your advert has appeared in the weekly *Trade Marks Journal*.

Legal protection

The law gives a period of protection that can range from five years to 50 years after your death. In practice, however, your only redress in the case of an infringement is through the courts, and that can be expensive.

(14)

Finally

KEY POINTS
To sum up, if you want to turn your big idea into a successful business, stick to the following guidelines and you'll improve your chances.

Advance planning
A business plan and a realistic cash flow forecast are a must. Try setting targets for your business, daily if possible. That way you are able to adjust or make changes quickly before a minor problem becomes a full scale reason for failure.

Advice
Never has advice been so plentiful, and never has advice been of the quality available today from enterprise advisors, banks, libraries, web sites and a whole host of government bodies dedicated to your business success. Take that advice and tailor it to your business venture.

Location
Considered by the experts to be the single most important factor governing the success or failure of your business, particularly if you are a retailer. Take the time and trouble to find premises in the best location possible.

Bookkeeping

Tired after a hard day's work? Putting off doing the paperwork is a sure recipe for disaster. Remember the old saying 'Don't put off until tomorrow that which can be done today'! It must have been written with the small business in mind.

The competition

Forget customer loyalty – it is almost extinct. Customers will find the best product or service at the best price, so keep your eye on your competitors, try to stay ahead with your marketing, and don't be afraid to copy ideas (without infringing patents of course). If you are unable to market your product or service yourself bring in an expert to do it for you. Your local Enterprise Agency can help you to locate the right person for the job.

The customer

The customer is always right (not really but let them think they are.) Someone so hard to attract in the first place must be handled with kid gloves and treated with the utmost respect, for without them your business will perish and die.

Versatility

Jack of all trades and master of as many as possible – the more functions you yourself are capable of, the lower the running cost of your business. Work out the amount of profit on sales required to cover the cost of, say, employing a man to clean out a blocked drain, then do it yourself, it is a most satisfying exercise.

Employees

1. Employ the least number of people possible to achieve the desired result.

2. Ensure they are correctly trained.

3. Create an efficient and happy workplace.

4. Treat them with respect, whatever the level expected of them.

5. Be fair in disputes.

Cash flow problems

Keep a close eye on receipts and payments and check transactions daily. If you experience problems, don't stick your head in the sand – get advice.

Staying ahead of the game

Watch for changes in fashion, watch your competitors and be prepared to move with the times.

WHERE TO GET HELP

Listed in the following pages are names of organisations who may be of some assistance to you in the setting up and running of your business.

Good luck with your business and may you always be successful!

ACAS Reader Ltd, Publications are available on-line at www.acas.org.uk Tel: 01455 852225

Advertising Standards Authority (ASA), 2 Torrington Place, London WCIE 7HW. Tel: (020) 7580 5555. *www.asa.org.uk*

Advisory, Conciliation and Arbitration Service (ACAS), Brandon House, 180 Borough High Street, London SE1 1LW. Tel: 0845 7474747. *www.acas.gov.uk*

Association of British Insurers (ABI), 51 Gresham Street, London EC2V 7HQ. Tel: (020) 76000 3333. *www.a-bi.org.uk*

Bank of England, Issue Office, Threadneedle Street, London EC2R 8AH. Tel: (020) 7601 4444. *www.bankofengland.co.uk*

British Chamber of Commerce (BCC), Binley Business Park, Harry Weston Road, Coventry CV3 2UN. Tel: (024) 7665 4321. *www.cw-chamber.co.uk*

British Franchise Association (BFA), Thames View, Newtown Road, Henley-on-Thames RG9 1HG. Tel: (01491) 578050. *www.british-franchise.org*

British International Freight Association (BIFA), Redfurn House, Browells Lane, Feltham TW13 7EP. Tel: (020) 8844 2266. *www.bifa.org*

Chartered Institute of Patent Agents, 3rd Floor, 95 Chancery Lane, London WC2A 1DT. Tel: (020) 7405 9450. *www.cipa.org.uk*

Chartered Institute of Taxation, 12 Upper Belgrave Street, London SW1X 8BB. Tel: (020) 7235 9381. *www.tax.org.uk*

Commission for Racial Equality, St Dunstans House, 201–211 Borough High Street, London SE1 1GZ. Tel: (020) 7993 9000.

Companies House (England and Wales), Crown Way, Maindy, Cardiff CF4 3UZ. Tel: 0790 333363. *www.companieshouse.gov.uk*

Companies House (Scotland), 37 Castle Terrace, Edinburgh EH1 2EB. Tel: (0131) 535 5800. *www.companieshouse.gov.uk*

Companies Registry (Northern Ireland), IDB House, 64 Chichester Street, Belfast BT1 4JX. Tel: 0870 333363. *www.companieshouse.gov.uk*

Consumer Credit Trade Association, Suite 8, The Wool Exchange, 10 Hustlergate, Bradford BD1 1RE. Tel: 01274 390380. *www.ccta.co.uk*

Croner's Reference Book for Self Employed and Smaller Businesses, Croner House, 145 London Road, Kingston-upon-Thames KT2 6SR. Tel: (020) 8547 3333. *www.info@iba.org.uk*

Direct Marketing Association (UK) 70 Margaret Street, London W1W 8SS. Tel: (020) 7291 3300. *www.dma.org.uk*

DTI Consumer Affairs Division, Department of Trade and Industry, 1 Victoria Street, London SW1H OET. Tel: (020) 7215 5000. *www.dti.gov.uk*

DTI Consumer Safety Publications, Admail 528, London SW1W 8YT. Tel: 0870 150 2500. *www.dti.gov.uk*

DTI Loan Guarantee Unit, Department of Trade and Industry, Small Firms Division, Level 2, St Mary's House, c/o Moorfoot Sheffield S1 4PQ. Tel: 0845 0010032/0845 0010033. *www.dti.gov.uk*

English Partnerships, 110 Buckingham Palace Road, London SW1W 9SA. Tel: (020) 7881 1600. *www.englishpartnerships.co.uk*

Equal Opportunities Commission, Arndale House, Arndale Centre, Manchester M4 3EQ. Tel: 0845 6015901. *www.eoc.org.uk*

Federation of Small Businesses, Sir Frank Whittle Way, Blackpool Business Park, Blackpool, Lancashire FY4 2FE. Tel: (01253) 336000. *www.fsb.org.uk*

Finance and Leasing Association, 2nd Floor, Imperial House, 15–19 Kingsway, London WC2B 6UN. Tel: (020) 7836 6511. *www.fla.org.uk*

Financial Services Authority, 25 The North Colonnade, Canary Wharf, London E14 5HS. Tel: (020) 7066 1000. *www.fsa.gov.uk*

The Forum of Private Business Ltd, Ruskin Chambers, Drury Lane, Knutsford, Cheshire WA16 6HA. Tel: (01565) 634467. *www.fpb.co.uk*

Health and Safety Executive, Caerphilly Business Park, Caerphilly CF83 3GG. Tel: 08701 545500. *www.hse.gov.uk*

Instant Muscle (IM) Ltd, 115–123 Powis Street, Woolwich SE18 6JE. Tel: (020) 8319 5660. *www.CharitiesDirect.com*

Institute of Business Advisors, Response House, Queen Street North, Chesterfield, S41 9AB. Tel: (01246) 453 3322 *www.iba.org.uk*

Institute of Chartered Accountants in England and Wales, PO Box 433, Chartered Accountants Hall, Moorgate Place, London EC2P 2BJ. Tel: (020) 7920 8100. *www.icaew.co.uk*

Institute of Export, Export House, Minerva Business Park, Lynch Wood, Peterborough PE2 6FT. Tel: (01733) 404400. *www.export.org.uk*

Institute of Insurance, Highams Business Centre, Midlands Road, Highams Ferrers, Northamptonshire NN10 8DW. Tel: (01933) 410 003. *www.inst.ins.brokers@iib-uk.com*

Insurance Brokers Registration Council, Higham Business Centre, Midland Road, Higham Ferrers, Northamptonshire NN10 8DW. Tel: (01933) 410003. *www.iib-uk.com*

International Chamber of Commerce (UK), 12 Grosvenor Place, London SW1X 7HH. Tel: (020) 7838 9363. *www.iccuk.net*

Mailing Preference Service, Haymarket House, 1 Oxendon Street, London SW1Y 4EE. Tel: (01673) 859100. *www.admar.co.uk*

National Computing Centre, Oxford House, Oxford Road, Manchester M1 7ED. Tel: (0161) 242 2121. *www.ncc.co.uk*

National Newspapers Mail Order Protection Scheme Ltd, 18a King Street, Maidenhead SL6 1EF. Tel: (01628) 641930. *www.mops.org.uk*

NCM Credit Insurance, 3 Harbour Drive, Capital Waterside, Cardiff CF1 6TZ. Tel: (029) 20 824000. *www.altradius.com*

Office of Fair Trading, 15–25 Bream's Buildings, London EC4A 1PR. Tel: 0845 7224499. *www.oft.gov.uk*

Office of Fair Trading, Consumer Credit Licensing Branch, Craven House, 40 Uxbridge Road, London W5 2BS. Tel: 0845 7224499. *www.oft.gov.uk*

Office of Fair Trading Publications, Fleetbank House, 2–6 Salisbury Square, London EC4 8JX. Tel: (020) 7221 8000. *www.oft.gov.uk*

Office of the Data Protection Register, Atradius, 3 Harbour Drive, Capital Waterside, Cardiff CF10 4WZ. Tel: 0870 2437788. *www.atradius.com*

Patents Office, Cardiff Road, Newport NP10 8QQ. Tel: 08459 500 505. *www.patent.gov.uk*

The Prince's Youth Business Trust, 18 Park Square East, London NW1 4LH. Tel: (020) 7321 6500. *www.pybt.-com*

South East England Development Agency, SEEDA, Cross Lanes, Guildford GU1 1YA. Tel: (01483) 484200. *www.seeda.co.uk*

Surrey Business Enterprise Agency, 19a High Street, Woking, Surrey GU21 6BW. Tel: (01483) 728434. *www.sbe.org.uk*

Technical Help to Exporters, British Standards Institution Information Centre, 389 Chiswick Road, London W4 4AL. Tel: (020) 8996 9000. *www.bsiglobal.com*

Telephone Preference Service, Haymarket House, 1 Oxendon Street, London SW1Y 4EE. Tel: (020) 7291 3320. *www.tpsonline.org.uk*

Thomson Directories, Customer Care Department, 70 Margaret Street, London W1W 8SS. Tel: (01252) 555 555. *www.thompsondirectories.com*

Trade Indemnity plc, 1 Canada Square, Canary Wharf, London E14 5DX. Tel: (020) 7512 9333. *www.eulerhermes.us/uk*

Glossary

Advertising. The communication of a sales message.

Agent. A person or business that sells goods or services, on behalf of another person or business.

Assembly. The process of joining parts together to make a project or part of a product.

Bargain. An agreement between negotiating partners.

Bonuses. Extra payment, generally given on a target achievement.

Bought ledger. A record of a business purchase.

Brand name. A well known name for a product or group of products.

Business options. Alternative choices a business can make.

Business plan. A complete written business scheme that gives financial and personal details normally required by banks or other financial institutions when asked to provide finance.

Business policy. The way in which the business operates.

Business rates. The tax levied on a business property.

Buyers. Those who make the decision to buy.

Capital equipment. Equipment purchased for the business, and the cost is recovered over a number of years.

Cash and carry. As it implies, you pay for your goods in cash (or cheque by arrangement) and take them away.

Cash flows. The flow of money in and out of the business.

Commission. A payment based on a person's results.

Competitive advantage. A product or service perceived by the customer to be better from one supplier than the competition.

Components. A part of a larger product.

Consumer. The end user of the product.

Contract. A written, spoken or implied agreement.

Cost plus. Used to work out a price, (cost plus profit).

Credit. Scheduled payment after receipt of the goods.

Credit note. Document given to a customer or given to you by a supplier to adjust for invoicing errors or return of faulty goods which shows they are in credit to a certain amount.

Customer. The person who exchanges money for goods or services on sale.

Delivery note. Lists the goods delivered. Must be signed by the purchaser or an agent. One copy is retained by the supplier, the other copy goes with the goods.

Delivery point. The place to which the goods are delivered.

Direct mail. Mail sent direct to the customer.

Discount. A reduction in the price, offered as an incentive to purchase.

Financing costs. Interest charges paid to the lender by the borrower, for goods purchased.

Gross margin. The profit from a sale, excluding overheads, but including any costs related to the product.

Hiring. The use of goods, without ownership for money.

Invoice. A written total of a purchaser's debt.

Leasing. A long-term contract, allowing use of equipment for a scheduled sum of money.

Letterheads. Name, address and other details, written or printed on correspondence paper.

Mainsheets. Advertising materials sent by post.

Market. An area of demand for a product or service.

Market research. To collate market information.

Media. Outside organisations such as the press, TV and radio, that allow advertising.

Merchandising material. Advertising material generally to be found at the point of sale.

Objections. Raised by the customer, can be overcome by the trained sales person.

Order processing. A system for the handling of orders to ensure efficient service.

Overdraft facility. A bank service that allows your account to go into the red, up to an arranged limit.

Overheads. Costs to a business other than direct product costs.

Over trading. Cash input rate is unable to finance increases in orders.

Performance. Reality as opposed to forecasts.

Pilot. A test scheme, allowing a length of time to investigate the public's reaction to your planned business, in a small controlled way.

Planning permission. The legal permission to erect, alter, or change the use of a building.

Product. The saleable item.

Product lines. A range of saleable items.

Promotion. An all-embracing marketing tool.

Promotional literature. Brochures, leaflets and other printed material.

Prospects. A possible customer.

Public relations. Influencing others to communicate and to promote your goods or services.

Quotation. An estimate of cost or quantity.

Remuneration. Payment by way of cash, goods, or benefits to an employee.

Repeat orders. Orders that follow the first order.

Retailing. The process of selling direct to the customer.

Sale or return. A sales method that allows the customer to test the goods, and then decide whether to buy them or return them.

Sales control. A method of control that requires sales staff to report to management, to ensure that sales efforts are correctly distributed.

Sales forecast. Used as a tool for the forward planning for financial, and manpower movement.

Sales promotion. The planned push to sell.

Samples. A form of sales promotion, a give-away to encourage purchase.

Service. After-sales care or maintenance, is an excellent sales feature.

Service levels. A measure of service.

Sole trader. A business owned by one person, as opposed to a partnership or limited company.

Sponsorship. A form of advertising. Money is given by commercial companies to pay the costs of sports events, or to finance an individual, or team, in exchange for allowing the company to advertise goods or services.

Statutory. A law created by a legislature.

Stock control. A method of checking stock for the purpose of maintaining the correct level.

Strategy. The method of using finance to achieve the best results.

Strengths. The good qualities of a business.

Subcontractor. A business employed by another business, to complete a job or contract.

System. A group of related activities, turning known inputs into results.

Targets. A set point at which to direct effort.

Technical support. Technical service and help to support a product or service.

Threats. Events outside the control of the business that may adversely affect its trade.

Trade paper. A special journal for a specific trade.

Trading. Selling goods purchased at a lower price.

Utilities. Electricity, gas, etc.

Wholesaling. To sell for resale.

Working capital. Money needed to pay running costs prior to receiving income revenue.

Zero options. No choice.

Index